LADY
OF THE
TBOLI

LADY
OF THE
TBOLI

DORIS FELL

CHRISTIAN HERALD BOOKS
Chappaqua, New York

Library of Congress Cataloging in Publication Data

Fell, Doris Elaine.
   Lady of the Tboli.

    1. Forsberg, Vivian.   2. Lindquist, Alice.
3. Missionaries—United States—Biography.
4. Missionaries—Philippine Islands—Biography.
5. Missions to Tboli (Philippine people)   I. Title.
BV3382.A1F44   266'.009599'7   79-50950

ISBN 0-915684-28-4

Dedicated to
Little Mothers Everywhere
Especially
My Own and Viv's

TABLE OF CONTENTS

Prologue 9
1. Trouble on the Fringes 11
2. The Blue Grass Roots 21
3. Valley Among the Mountains 27
4. Picnic at the Hot Springs 33
5. All This—And Children Too 37
6. Breaking Patterns of the Past 41
7. Mountain Survey to a Man Named Doming 49
8. Myra Lou: Room 401 59
9. Back to Sinolon 65
10. In the Middle of Beginnings 73
11. At the House in Sinolon 77
12. The Mountain of Homesickness 83
13. Sleeping Nets and Gospel Checks 93
14. Pike's Peak—Short Cut to Triumph 99
15. The Kiamba Coastal Run 103
16. Scout's Honor 109
17. The House in the Gully 115
18. Fining's Little World 121
19. A Mountain Range Away 125
20. Ali's Little Red Book 131
21. Barefoot in the Palace 135
22. Blueprints to Change 141
23. The Blowing of the Wind 145
24. Flowers Around the Outhouse 149
25. The Echo of a Song 157
26. Church at the Mountaintop 167
27. Barrels Are for Packing 175
28. They Are My Glory 183
29. The Turning of the Pages 191
Epilogue 201

PROLOGUE

In 1953 Vivian Forsberg and Alice Lindquist, Wycliffe Bible translators in the Philippines, struck out across a roadless countryside, thick with cogon grass, to reach the Tboli mountain people with God's Good News.

Years later I visited their barrio in Sinolon and watched their New Testament translation unfolding in lives in a thatched, bamboo house bursting with boys and laughter. "Someday I'm going to write the Tboli story," I told Vivian.

She laughed—the writing seemed so far away—but she said, "When you do, write your book so that the struggle and the questions show through."

The cost of giving these people the Tboli New Testament was an upward climb most of the way. "But, God," the translators cried, prayed, "the stakes are high. There are endless, exhausting trails—the mountains are too steep. We can't climb them alone."

"I'll climb them with you," he replied.

Now and then the translators faced a valley, deep and painful. And sometimes a storm hit of typhoon size. But the twenty-five years that spanned the entry into Sinolon to the evacuation due to rebel uprising and the final return to the barrio saw God's Word speak Tboli.

When I asked the translation team, "What did it cost to give the Tboli the Scriptures?" they had difficulty pinpoint-

9

ing their answers. "How do you sum up twenty-odd years in a few words?" Viv responded thoughtfully. "In time? In lives? In obedience? In dollars?"

As I studied their story, I found my own answers. The stakes of Bible translation are always high. The Tboli New Testament comes at a price far greater than any human expenditure involved, for apart from the Man on the Cross—the Risen Savior—there would have been no translation, no story.

1
TROUBLE ON THE FRINGES

Rumors. Rebels. Restlessness.

Thoughts of all three needled slim, tawny-haired Vivian Forsberg as she sat at her typewriter. She sighed, rolled in three sheets of paper with carbons between, and typed "Sunday, 15 September 1974," then, "Dear Family." She pressed the return key on her Olympia and paused, wondering what to say to the people back home. Should she spread rumors any farther, alarming the family needlessly about Muslim insurgents in the valley?

She glanced at her partner, Marge Moran, who was also a Wycliffe translator. Marge leaned against the bamboo wall, sipping her breakfast coffee.

"I'm not sure what to write about," Viv complained.

"Do what I do," Marge answered. "Don't write. Or . . ." she said as she poured a second cup of coffee, "tell them about the weather." Marge motioned toward the skyline, visible through the open kitchen window.

Outside, early morning nimbus clouds rose in mists around the mountains in Upper Sinolon, Mindanao, shadowing the Philippine hillsides in velvety darkness. Above the mist, rain-laden streamers of charcoal gray moved relentlessly toward the village, toward the lone bamboo house in the cornfield where Vivian and Marge lived. A slight breeze whistled hauntingly through the bamboos. The women were accustomed to

11

sudden tropical storms, but just over the hillside a short distance to the east of the Sefali River, another thick cloud, worse than any thunderstorm, gathered momentum.

Beyond the thatched house the land climbed on all sides, first gently, then steeply into rugged hills and mountains full of Tboli people.

The Alah Valley with its surrounding mountains, its bright splashes of bougainvillea, and its random patches of corn-fields had been home for Vivian for more than twenty years. Viv and her three partners, all members of the Tboli transla-tion team, were determined to finish the job they started out to do. The Tboli people would have the New Testament in their own language.

"Fi iish your letter," Marge encouraged as she gathered up the breakfast dishes. "And while you're about it, throw in a carbon for me."

Viv smiled, turned her thoughts back to her family, and wrote, "It looks like a storm is moving our way...."

At midmorning Vivian was still at her typewriter when she heard the grinding roar of a plane overhead. It sounded as though the old twin-engine Baron was too tired to fight the wind. Moments later the *boom boom boom* and low rum-blings of spasmodic gunfire startled her. She paused in mid-sentence, her fingers tensed above the typing keys.

For the last two weeks, there had been an atmosphere of unreality in the valley. First there were rumors. "The black-shirts have arrived," one Tboli man had announced sadly. "They are coming in from the coast over the mountain ranges—five hundred strong with high-powered foreign rifles." The blackshirts were a band of rebel insurgents.

"There is heavy fighting to the southeast near Mt. Parker," another man added. "They are attacking first one barrio and then another. They are stealing, burning, killing."

Viv was sure the rebels had nothing against the Tboli people. Their conflict over land was with the lowlanders where the Tboli intermingled. But as the rumors spread, refugees streamed through the neighboring municipalities; the people in Viv's barrio at Sinolon were becoming more fearful with every passing day.

The Alah Valley where Viv and Marge lived ran southwest between the Alah and Sefali rivers. Over the years, as far back as Viv could remember, lowlanders had moved into the valley, claiming the land and pushing the Tboli mountain folk across the rivers and back up the mountainsides. But there had never been a threat of personal danger or rumors like the ones recently spreading through the valley.

Viv now listened intently, straining to distinguish the sounds of trouble. It was quiet again.

Promptly at 11:45 A.M. Viv left the unfinished correspondence and joined Marge for the "sked," the scheduled radio contact with Nasuli, the Wycliffe center on Mindanao. Viv stood by as Marge pressed the button on the microphone and spoke crisply into the set: "This is SIL Sinolon calling SIL Nasuli . . . we have news. We think we heard gunfire nearby this morning. . . ."

Associate Director Ed Ruch was on the receiving line. "That doesn't sound good," he said. "Would you like me to come and help you pack so you can fly out today?"

"We can't just walk out like that; we'll have to wait for the boys to come home," Marge replied.

Viv nodded agreement. The four Tboli boys who made their home with the translators during the school week had gone to their mountain homes for the weekend and would not be back until evening.

"You're scheduled out for the three-month workshop at Nasuli anyway," Ed quickly reminded them.

"I know," Marge's voice crackled back over the transmitter.

"But we don't look forward to another long absence from Sinolon. Why make it any longer than necessary?" Viv whispered from the sidelines. All week long, in spite of the rumors, Viv had been checking the translation of I Peter with Tboli who had never read it before, gathering data, correcting word usage, preparing material for the workshop in semantics and translation.

"We have some more language work to do and then we'll come out on Wednesday as planned," Marge promised.

Finally, Ed agreed. The team would put the finishing touches to I Peter and fly out to Nasuli in the middle of the week.

When the sked was over and the radio was silent, Viv and Marge looked at each other. Had they made the right decision? The situation wasn't good. Though the fighting had been confined to fringe areas east of them, it could change quickly and move in fast. They sat down at the large kitchen table, their arms resting on the yellow-and-white checked tablecloth, to talk, to pray.

"Lord, if you want us to get out our equipment on Monday—if that is your will—would you send Ethel over this afternoon?" Marge prayed.

Ethel Moorehouse, a friend with the Christian and Missionary Alliance Mission, would not routinely be in the area on Sunday, for she had a teaching commitment at Lake Sebu. If she came at all, it would be late afternoon before she arrived.

When the girls finished praying, Marge stood up wordlessly, pushed her dark-rimmed glasses back on the narrow bridge of her nose, and walked into her bedroom. She reached for her suitcase and started to pack. Viv went down the back steps and crossed the grounds to the one-room study house where they did most of their translation work. Reluctantly she began to pile translation materials into empty boxes.

They worked until late afternoon. By five, Ethel still had not come. The four boys—Nga To', Min, Gadu, and Igi—had arrived home from the mountains and already Igi, the high schooler, was on his way back to King's Institute for another week of study.

Just before dusk, Ethel stopped her blue Toyota pickup truck in the front yard.

"Did you hear the noise this morning?" Viv called, approaching the truck.

"Your noise," Ethel responded loudly, "was a strafing raid in the mountains." She went on to explain that according to rumor the Philippine Air Force had made a reconnaissance flight over the rebel encampment. The rebels fired, damaging the plane.

"I've moved my valuables to Surala in case we have to evacuate," Ethel told them, blotting her forehead with a hanky. "I'll be glad to help you move your things there."

Viv moaned. "Do you realize we have a whole bodega full of Tboli books... not to mention the Scripture portions we've just translated, and hymnbooks, cassette recorders...."

"And crate after crate of primers and supplementary readers," joined in Marge.

"You know the rebels' pattern is loot and burn," Ethel reminded them. "You can replace your own things, but do you want twenty-two years of language work to go up in smoke?"

There was no question now as to the necessity of storing their equipment in a safer place. They would pack the rest of their literacy materials and send them out with Ethel in the morning.

Marge was up early, stuffing the linens into the gas-engined washing machine. As the clothes spun, the team put in an emergency call to Nasuli for a cargo flight. They planned to send out everything of importance from the study house—translation materials, favorite commentaries, typewriters.

After a breakfast of rice and dried fish, Viv and Marge

watched Nga To', their third grader, slick down his black hair, toss his school bag over his shoulder, and trudge off toward the barrio school, his sturdy legs carrying him down the path through the cornfields. To' was the youngest and the last of twenty boys or more—they'd almost lost count—who had made their home with the translators.

To' had hardly disappeared from view when Bedung, a short, stocky young man who had been one of their first boys to leave the house and marry, came riding up on his horse. "I had a feeling you would need my help today," he told them.

Twenty-two-year-old Gadu, their chief translation helper, nodded from the bamboo porch. "We need your help, friend," he greeted Tboli-fashion. Then, using the special names for the two translators, he said, "Ye' Udi and Ye' Li are packing." He came down the steps, his face clouded, his mood far from his usual happy-go-lucky attitude for which he had been nicknamed "Peter Rabbit."

Bedung looked questioningly from Gadu to the translators. Hadn't they left many times before? He frowned, beads of perspiration still dotting his upper lip and spreading across his wide, flat nose. "It is safer if you go?" he asked simply, knowingly.

As Bedung helped Marge in the house, Gadu took his place beside Viv in the bodega (storeroom). Together, silently pulling and pushing, tugging and heaving, they moved the boxes of primers and workbooks. Viv and Gadu had difficulty finding the right boards to go on the heavy boxes, just as they were having difficulty with words. Neither of them could say how they really felt inside.

To Vivian, Gadu was like a well-kept volcano, rumbling, explosive, momentarily about to erupt. She knew he was frustrated with the whole situation—the fighting, the uncertain future, and especially with their leaving.

"And how are you going to nail these covers on?" Gadu

asked in exasperation. "There are no nails the proper size, not even an old, rusty one." He looked around and scooped up a bent, discarded nail he had pulled from the boards. He swung the hammer, whacking his left thumb in the process. Gadu slammed the hammer to the floor and glared angrily at Viv.

She stared back in silence. He had barely missed the family of three kittens chasing one another around the boxes. Viv scooped up the nearest kitten and petted it affectionately. "We've got to find a nail for Gadu and find it fast," she told the bit of silver gray fluff.

The parakeet chirped brightly in his nearby cage. But Snoopy, their wheat-colored German shepherd, crept over and licked Gadu's hand, his tail wagging restlessly. A twisted grin spread slowly over Gadu's bony cheeks as he leaned down and scratched Snoopy's ears.

At 9 A.M. that morning, while Ethel and the Tboli team loaded the heavy boxes into the Toyota, Dave King and Ed Warnock, JAARS pilots with Wycliffe, took off from Nasuli in the Helio Courier RP 39. After making two scheduled stops, they reached Sinolon at 11:15. Everything was quiet. The sun was shining, the wind rustling pleasantly. The "war troubles" seemed far away.

After loading 609 pounds of valuable cargo into the plane, the pilots turned to Viv. "We'll be back with the Piper Super Cub on Wednesday to pick you up for workshop," Dave told her. Then with Dave, a former Air Force pilot, at the controls, the cargo plane lifted and headed for Nasuli.

Viv and Marge returned to packing, storing most of their cooking utensils into large drums in the study—the only place where they could hook the bamboo shutters and lock the door. Finally Viv crawled around behind the desk and unhooked the speaker from the battery-run record player. As she took the speaker down, Gadu glared intently. "You're not taking that now, too, are you?" he asked softly.

Viv's voice was strained. "We can't leave it for the rebels to destroy, Gadu."

The young man's eyes filled with unspoken disappointment. "So when you go now—you're not coming back?"

"Of course we're coming back." The look on both their faces only added a question mark to her answer.

While rice and vegetables simmered on the wood-burning stove, Viv and Marge carried the final load of boxes out to Ethel's truck. The truck was almost loaded when Ma' Singgung, a Tboli man from the other side of the Sefali River, came running up the dirt road, his body dripping with sweat, his bare back glistening. "The blackshirts have arrived at the Father of Flidu's place, just over the first mountain from the market. Everyone is leaving." Ma' Singgung sucked in his breath before adding, "It's the mountain just beyond Bedung's place." He shot a quick glance at Bedung and shrugged helplessly.

"Min and Nga To's families live there," Viv exclaimed. She leaned against the Toyota, her eyes wide with disbelief. The three women looked knowingly at one another. The insurgents were smack in the middle of Tboli country and headed their way.

"Is it true, friend?" Gadu asked as he straddled a rolled mattress, tying it securely, the muscles of his arms bulging.

"It is true," Ma' Singgung assured him.

Gadu's brown, almond-shaped eyes darkened. He laughed a dry, ironic laugh and said, "It's happened then. It's arrived." It was Gadu's way of saying, "War has come."

Although it was unlike Tboli to leave in haste, on hearing the news, Bedung ran for his horse. With hardly a word of farewell, he galloped away. His wife and child lived in the barrio just across the Sefali River.

Marge left her stunned companions and rushed into the house to call Nasuli. Because Dave and Ed were still in flight, forty-five minutes airborne, Marge's call crackled through.

"It looks like we'd better fly out today," she told them.

Without waiting for lunch, Ethel and three Tboli helpers left in the Toyota truck. The road veered in the direction where the rebels were reportedly moving. When she reached the barrio of Edwards, the main road was blocked with people and belongings, everyone looking for a ride. Ethel stopped at her own house by the market and picked up her co-worker Aning, then moved out once again for the safety of Surala, the boys clinging to the back of the truck.

Back in Sinolon, Nga To' was just getting home from school. The house was almost bare. It had looked ordinary when he left that morning, but now he had come home to a different, empty world. To' stopped, rocked to a halt on his thongs, and gazed from one to the other, his eyes finally resting on Viv. He looked at her squarely, his brown eyes big as saucers. "But I thought you weren't leaving until Wednesday," he challenged.

Things had happened too quickly for Nga To'. Too quickly for Viv. She couldn't find the words to answer him. How could she explain that the boys belonged with their own mountain families? They could not go with Viv and Marge.

At one o'clock Ed Warnock's wife met him at the airstrip at Nasuli with a peanut-butter sandwich and a hug. Immediately, Ed crawled into the Piper Super Cub, *The Spirit of Rockford,* adjusted his safety straps and earphones, and took off, alone, for the flight back to Sinolon.

At 2:15 Ed landed the plane on the Sinolon strip, the dust flying as he skidded to a stop. Viv, the perennial optimist, knew now how it felt to be running out when the going got rough. It was against everything she believed in as she turned to three of the boys with last-minute instructions. "Run if there's any sign of trouble at all," she urged.

"Leave the house if the fighting gets close," Marge added. "Don't guard anything. Run to the mountains."

Then Viv turned away hurriedly and crawled into the

remodeled back seat of the Super Cub. Ed tightened the
seat strap for her before balancing the birdcage with the pale
blue parakeet on her lap. As Marge settled in the seat
directly in front of her, Vivian glanced out the window.
Gadu, Min, and Nga To' stood on the airstrip with Snoopy
beside them, wagging his tail.

As the red and white plane lifted off the ground, its wing
dipping in salute, Viv and Marge couldn't hold back the
tears, and tears were still there when they arrived at Nasuli.
As they stepped from *The Spirit of Rockford* into the afternoon sun, they were met by many missionary colleagues.
Marge and Viv could talk only about their dilemma of leaving the boys and the Tboli people. Viv's voice was choked
with emotion, apology. "We can get in a plane and fly
away," she said. "But what about the Tboli?"

2
THE BLUE
GRASS ROOTS

Vivian Forsberg grew up in a small farming community in Blue Grass, Minnesota, the third of five children. Blue Grass was just a spot on the road, halfway between Sebeka and Wadena in central Minnesota. Besides the Forsberg's general store, where her father and uncle sold everything from spuds to hardware, there were a gasoline station and two churches—the Catholic church with the steeple and the Lutheran church the Forsbergs attended.

The security of Viv's Scandinavian homelife and the spontaneous laughter in the Forsberg household were happy preparations for missionary service. Viv couldn't remember any Christmas more special than those at home with the family nor any part of growing up more exciting than winning 4-H Club prizes at the Wadena County Fair.

When Viv was a thirteen-year-old high school freshman, cousins invited her to their Sunday evening service at the church in Wadena. While the congregation sang a hymn on heaven, the pastor said, "Now all of you stand who can sing, 'Yes, my name's written there.'"

Everyone around her stood. Viv tried to stand, too, but her feet were like lead. *I've gone to church and Sunday school all my life,* she thought defensively, *and won prizes for memorizing Bible verses.* But inside she knew she had never had a definite encounter with God, never really talked with him about becoming part of his family.

Anger mingled with her new discovery. *I'm just as good as my cousins. When I get out of here,* she promised herself as she gripped the hymnbook, *I'll never come back. Never. Never.*

"Never" lasted five years. On her first Christmas vacation from Staples Normal School, the same cousins invited Viv for the weekend. That Sunday morning, as Viv heard her cousins' pastor preach, the Christmas message became real to her. She was finally ready to obey Christ, ready to be part of the family of God.

In 1944, after three years of teaching in a one-room school and shortly after breaking her engagement to a seminary student, Viv left home and the Blue Grass country for the Lutheran Deaconess Hospital in Minneapolis to fulfill her lifelong goal of becoming a nurse.

Beatrice Long, Vivian's roommate at nursing school, planned on going abroad as a missionary. In their junior year, during coffee hour one evening, Viv talked with a missionary guest from Madagascar.

"After we graduate, my roommate is going to the Orient as a missionary," Viv announced enthusiastically.

"Oh," the senior missionary responded. "Tell me about it."

Morris Wagner listened quietly to Viv's description, an amused smile curling at the corners of his mouth. He took it all in and then he said, "And what about you, Vivian?"

A bite-size piece of cake balanced on Vivian's fork. "Oh, no," she answered, her eyes sparkling with her own dream. "After graduation I'm going back and work with the young people in my home church."

Morris Wagner smiled. "I see," he said gently. But Viv never quite forgot his asking, *And what about you?*

During that same year at Deaconess, alone in the dorm one morning, Viv met a new challenge. She was sitting crosslegged on her bed, her Bible in her lap, trying to puzzle

out what God had in mind in the book of Hebrews. Suddenly the book became personal, the message clear. God was
asking her to be a missionary, too. The idea was startling.

Viv looked up in the empty room. "But what about my
family, Lord?" she asked aloud.

God's answer was just as clear as if she heard the words
audibly. "I'll take care of your family." Tears were already
sneaking over the brim, trickling down her cheeks, dropping
their stains on her wrinkled uniform and pinafore apron.
Then and there she slipped off her bed and knelt beside it,
sealing that agreement—willingly, lovingly promising to
obey. "I'll go anywhere, do anything you ask me to do,
Lord, if you'll take care of my family."

Viv began to name them, one by one.

When she stood up and glanced at her watch, there was
just enough time to dash off a letter to Mom and Dad to tell
them of her decision. As she crossed the street to the hospital she was more lighthearted and joyful than she had ever
been in her life. She was the Lord's completely, without
reservation. His promise to her regarding her family was as
real as if it had already happened. Without knowing it, Viv
had made the first payment on the cost of the Tboli New
Testament. She had personally committed herself to God to
go anywhere and do anything.

In 1948, a year after graduating from Deaconess Hospital, Viv enrolled at the Prairie Bible Institute in Alberta,
Canada. At Prairie, Viv heard chapel speaker Herbert
Whealey tell of a growing breed of missionary linguists
known as the Wycliffe Bible Translators, men and women
committed to putting God's Word into unwritten languages.
Viv responded, but after personally talking with the Wycliffe
translator, Viv returned to her room feeling inadequate for
such a task. She declared practically to her roommate, "I'm
not smart enough to be a Bible translator. I'm just going to
the mission field and nurse sick Indians."

Nevertheless, the challenge of Bible translation was there. She would never quite get away from it.

By the summer of 1951, Viv was already in her second year at the Summer Institute of Linguistics (SIL), this time at Norman, Oklahoma, preparing to be one of that special breed of missionary linguists. In midsummer, Dr. Richard Pittman, newly appointed director of the Wycliffe Far East advance, stopped Vivian on the campus. "Vivian, have you ever considered going to the Philippines?" he asked in his soft-spoken manner.

"I'm going to Peru and set up my own clinic," she responded, her face glowing enthusiastically. "As a nurse," she added for clarification.

"I see." Dick Pittman studied her from behind rimless glasses, his thin face serious. "We need more recruits—translators—for the Asian advance," he went on. "You will think about it, pray about it, won't you?" he urged kindly.

Viv was at a rare loss for words. Dick and Kay Pittman were two of her favorite Wycliffe people. She would gladly go to Timbuktu with them. But the Philippines? Dick was still studying her face, waiting quietly for her response.

She nodded. "I'll pray about it," she promised vaguely. But even as she said the words her thoughts were still on Peru, that South American country where so many of her friends were going.

She turned away from Dick, her smile hazy, and hurried to the small room on campus that served as the SIL library. She paused in the open doorway, aware of the roar of the large fan blowing against the Oklahoma heat. Fellow students were scattered around the room, bent over their study books. Viv moved quietly toward the large globe in the corner of the room. She twirled it, spinning it hurriedly by Peru, searching for the Philippine Islands. She kept looking around Hawaii. Finally, she found it—a stretch of islands like small dots on the globe far across the Pacific in the Asian world. Inside, she suddenly tingled with excitement, with expectation. Wycliffe had gained a new recruit for the Philippines.

It would be twenty months before negotiations with the Philippines would be finalized, allowing Viv to join twenty-one other young translators for assignment there. Bible translation would cost her discipleship. In her prayer letter before sailing she wrote, "But should I offer to the Lord that which cost me nothing? Lack I anything? Nothing. Save a visa."

"We've already prayed you across the Pacific," friends wrote back in April 1953 just before Viv and Alice Lindquist, a classmate from Bible school, boarded the American Mail Line freighter, the *S.S. Java Mail*, in Seattle, Washington.

On 13 May 1953, after twenty-seven days at sea, the *Java Mail* docked at pier 9 in Manila. Viv and Alice awakened at daybreak; the ship's engines were silent. "We're here," Viv said, balancing on her knees and peeking out the porthole above her bunk. The ship was bobbing slightly in the water. She stared somberly at the hulls of forty-six half-sunken ships that lay in the harbor, grim reminders of a long and costly war.

Minutes later, as Viv studied the mountainous coastline of the Philippines, a riot of color and cloud formations filled the sky. Just beyond the ship, jeepneys—remodeled American jeeps—lined the dock, waiting to carry the passengers into the heart of Manila.

Viv's dream had been to go to the mission field "just to nurse sick Indians." But God had other plans. All along he had been preparing a Bible translator. The Blue Grass roots of Minnesota were an ocean away now. Viv was about to dig new roots, to settle into life in a new country among a new people, the Tboli.

3
VALLEY AMONG THE MOUNTAINS

By the time the *Java Mail* anchored in Manila Bay, Dick Pittman had already signed the agreement between the Republic of the Philippines and the Summer Institute of Linguistics, opening the way for the Wycliffe advance in the Pacific. Surveys of language areas, including the Tboli, had been permitted, and SIL was ready to allocate the new translators at once. Shortly after Viv and Alice arrived in Manila, SIL assigned them to the Tboli. The new translators liked the sound of those plans.

An estimated forty thousand Tboli lived in south central Mindanao, a day or two from the coast, far south, high in the mountains of Cotabato Province. Little was known about them except that their contact with the outside world was limited. They had no written language, and they did not have the knowledge of a risen, returning Lord. That was enough to make Viv and Alice glad to go to them.

Translator Len Newell would leave his own family on Luzon and accompany the girls to the barrio of Sinolon to help them set up housekeeping. In July the three translators rode through the jeepney-swarming streets in Manila to the harbor, where they boarded an interisland boat for Mindanao. Two-foot-wide army cots lined the upper deck with only a canvas roof shielding them from the stars. As the *Snug Hitch* left Manila Bay, the sweltering heat of Manila

was left behind. But an army of flies tagged along. Like
people, the flies were thick.

Just past dusk, the three translators settled down dubiously in their street clothes to sleep. They lay flat on their backs,
staring blankly at the canvas ceiling, fighting cultural shock
as all around them men changed into pajamas and women
slipped into their nighties.

Viv was almost dozing when husky, red-haired Len re-
marked meekly, "I haven't any place to put my arms." Viv
giggled contagiously. In the middle of her laughter, she
slapped a pesky, inquisitive fly. Quickly she tucked the sheet
around her head and curled her own thin body comfortably
on the army cot. Then, still smiling at Len's remark, she fell
asleep.

She awakened the next morning to the voice of a steward
who stood by her cot, holding a tray full of cups. "Would
you like some coffee, Mum?" the steward asked, his wide,
bronzed face breaking readily into a smile.

Viv looked past the steward and noted the two long lines
of humanity waiting at the bathroom doors. She shrugged,
then reached for a cup of coffee. What the *Snug Hitch*
lacked in privacy, the people more than made up for in
friendliness.

Moments later, Viv sat by the ship's rail, sipping her
coffee, gazing at the mountainous coastline of Cebu. The
deep blue ocean beneath her was just rough enough to be
interesting, the skyline translucent blue. Filipinos gathered
around her, smiling and talkative.

"You are Americans?" one heavyset man asked.

"I am," Viv answered. "My friends are from Canada."

To the older man it made no difference. With World War II
obviously still fresh in his mind, he was full of praise for all
North Americans, especially the American soldiers. "Your
boys fought hard beside our boys and died with them," he
said, quietly reminiscing. His gratitude, like that of many on
board the *Snug Hitch*, extended to the missionaries.

There would be much for Viv to learn of this country, a country only seven years independent and still in the throes of a rebuilding program. But what Viv saw, she liked. She glanced across at Alice, who was sitting on a nearby bench. Viv smiled; Alice was deep in conversation with another Filipino.

Thursday evening, days after leaving Manila, the *Snug Hitch* finally docked. They traveled five kilometers inland by bus, and Viv and Alice made last-minute purchases.

"We still need a wash basin," Alice told Len.

"And a pail and drum of kerosene," Viv added, checking off each item as they made their selections.

While they continued their shopping, Len contacted the director of LASEDECO regarding their entry into Sinolon. LASEDECO, the Land Settlement and Development Company, was a governmental agency opening up Mindanao to lowland settlers. After obtaining a letter of introduction from the director, the trio traveled by truck over the winding, dusty road and deep gullies to Banga, the nearest mail town to Sinolon. The truck was almost a stranger to brakes, but the driver made it through the river and rocked them on to Banga, where Len presented their letter of introduction to Captain de la Cuesta, the LASEDECO director in Banga.

Next morning the captain, a veteran of the guerrilla warfare on Luzon, arranged for a weapons carrier to take the three translators and their three fifty-gallon kerosene drums full of supplies the rest of the way to Sinolon.

"I'm sorry the seats aren't more comfortable," he apologized as he helped the translators into straight-backed chairs in the back of the weapons carrier.

Viv tucked her cotton dress around her legs. She frowned sheepishly at her bobby socks and saddle shoes, wondering briefly whether she would have made a better impression with nylons or slacks for her grand entry into Sinolon. As she snickered at the thought, the driver, with Captain de la

Cuesta beside him, struck out across the roadless countryside thick with cogon grass. As the vehicle bounced them
over the rolling hills of the Alah Valley, the tips of their head
scarves and loose strands of hair blew in the breezes.

At the foot of the mountains, the driver lurched to a stop,
the brakes screeching in retaliation. "This is Sinolon," he
announced, wiping his sticky, dusty hands on his trouser
legs.

The translators looked around, marveling. The little barrio of Sinolon—with three kapok trees, several low palms,
and a handful of thatched houses—sat on the fringe of
civilization. In one direction were the lowlanders. And in the
hills were the isolated Tboli.

The Datu, or town mayor, who had previously promised
Wycliffe that the Tboli would have a place for the translators, was not at home. It was obvious that the Tboli had not
really expected the girls to come. The people appeared
from nowhere, staring shyly at the new arrivals.

"Where is Datu Edwards?" the captain asked them.

"In the fields," one man answered.

"Then send for him," the captain ordered. Soon the beat
of the drums was calling the Datu home from his fields.

While Len and the girls balanced on the Datu's ladder
steps, waiting for his arrival, the Datu's four wives shut the
door emphatically. Behind the cracks in the bamboo wall,
the translators could hear giggling and feminine whispers in
a language strange and musical to their ears. Alice, her
kerchief still knotted under her chin, turned around and
grinned at one of the cracks in the wall. There was another
burst of giggling from inside.

Viv smiled. "I wonder how long it will be before the Tboli
open their homes and their lives to us?" she asked.

Finally, Datu Piang Edwards, a short, wiry man educated
by an American army officer, arrived. He moved with confidence. In the weeks that would follow, Viv and Alice would

come to understand the reasons for his confidence. He had a thousand mountain people under his authority. He had taught them the value of abaca fiber and the sacks of rice which they used to barter for salt, horses, and cloth. Ma' Flidu, the "Father of Flidu," as the Datu was also known, encouraged his people to send their children down from their mountain homes to school. Books were important to him, and the translators were there to make books for his people.

Those who gathered with the Datu eyed the newcomers with suspicion. "What about these Melikan Bukay—these two white Americans?" they asked. "Have they come to take more of our land from us?"

"No," the Datu answered. "They do not want our land. They are here to learn the language. They want to give you books to read—books that will take the darkness out of your lives."

Captain de la Cuesta took the housing situation into his own hands. "These girls can't put out a lot of money on materials and labor for a house," he said. "Why can't you put up a house for them, Ma' Flidu? Could you get your men together and do that?"

The Datu agreed. "As soon as the new schoolhouse is built, my men will make them a house. Until then they may live there." He pointed with his chin toward the old school-house.

The translators followed his direction, three pairs of eyes solemnly studying the old building.

"Quaint," Alice said.

"It's split-level," Len commented dryly.

"It's got possibilities," Viv defended, studying the lower side with its shedlike addition. "That is, if the colt moves out."

They walked to the building with the Datu. He nudged the colt as they entered.

"Terrific. No scrubbing," Alice said cheerfully as she discovered the dirt flooring.

Their new home had big windows with no shutters and a large doorframe with no door. Everyone was welcome to walk right in. The chickens walked in. The dogs walked in. And so did the timid mountain people. For Viv and Alice there was no faster way to become acquainted with the Tboli than by living on their main thoroughfare.

The rest of the schoolhouse with its high ceiling made an excellent carpentry shop for Len and gave him a place to stay. As Len worked in his shop the people came, bringing papaya, bananas, corn, yams, and cassava, a root much like a sweet potato.

Days later one man said, "You will never grow hungry, friends, now that we know you eat our food."

The only thing they lacked was meat. There was none at all.

Before the week was up Len used the lumber and nails from packing crates to make a cupboard, a large medicine cabinet, three stools, and a cooler with wet gunny sack walls that kept food surprisingly cool. Alice and Viv assisted by painting their new furniture white and lining the shelves with red-edged shelf paper from their barrels.

The new furniture, complete with shiny red handles, was moved into place and arranged so as to avoid the leaks in the roof. One packing box contained a little portable organ, which soon found its spot in the house. Since Viv could play only hymns, a new type of melody filled the air at Sinolon.

4

PICNIC AT
THE HOT SPRINGS

All during that first week, Tboli visitors talked about the hot springs three mountains away, where the water bubbled out of the ground "so hot you couldn't put your foot in it." For the Tboli, the mountains were their world and the hot springs their greatest tourist attraction.

"You must see them," the people urged.

"It will only take three hours to get there," the Datu assured them.

From the open window in the schoolhouse the mountains didn't look high or far away. By 6:30 Sunday morning the sky had cleared from the Saturday rain, and the rookie recruits in Bible translation set out with a picnic lunch for the hot springs. The Datu and several Tboli traveled with them, a dozen hikers in all.

They walked for an hour on the slippery trail through tall cogon grass, sharp-edged against their bare arms and legs. "We should have worn slacks," Viv whispered, staring down at her scratched legs.

"They're not acceptable," returned Alice.

"A perfect homestead for gnats," Len complained, scratching through his trouser legs.

Halfway up the first mountain Alice stopped. "Let's turn back," she begged.

The narrow trail was as steep as it was slippery. But they

needed an open door with the people. "It's just three mountains away," Len reminded them.

They kept climbing.

Their guides, sure-footed as mountain goats, bounded up the slopes on bare, calloused feet. The muscles in the calves of their legs bulged as they hiked. Behind them, the rookies sloshed through the mud—Viv in the lead tugging at Alice's hand, Len pushing from behind.

"Medel," said one of the Tboli sympathetically.

"Slippery," interpreted the Datu in English.

"Hitok," offered another Tboli.

"Muddy," interpreted the Datu.

"Narrow," grumbled Alice, losing her footing and curling her toes in her mud-caked tennis shoes. Usually quiet and gentle-spirited, Alice had lost her enthusiasm for the picnic at the hot springs. Finally she stopped again, reached down wearily, and removed her shoes, pulling them carefully over her blistered heels. Tying them around her waist, she wiped the back of her hand over her forehead and pushed on barefoot behind Viv.

"I'm getting a better grip on the trail now," she declared. With those words of encouragement, it wasn't long before Len removed his tennis shoes. In time Viv, too, kicked off her two-tone saddles.

"It's just a short trip more," the Datu said patiently as he stopped along the trail and waited for the translators. "You can leave your shoes at that house." He pointed ahead to a small Tboli shack set back from the trail.

After leaving their shoes they hiked on, sticky and trail-worn. Up the rest of the first mountain slope, down the other side. Up the second mountain, down again. New blisters. New bruises.

Viv struggled on, her body bent forward, her eyes on the heels of the hiker in front of her. She sighed with exhaustion.

It was obvious to her now that to the Tboli, distance was measured by mountains. But she and her sunburned Canadian friends still measured distance by city blocks.

Finally, at noon, they spotted the springs. Hot water bubbled and steamed out of the ground in several places, then trickled slowly down the mountainside. "It's kind of pretty," Viv said as she surveyed the sulfur rock formations, her nose twitching against the smell.

The Datu ignored their disappointment. "During the war the Japanese wanted to use the sulfur for ammunition," he explained enthusiastically. "So the United States guarded this area from them." The sulfur fumes that clutched at the throats of the translators seemed hardly worthy of military recognition.

In the middle of their picnic lunch, large drops of rain splattered on them. "Not a rainstorm," groaned Len. He scrambled to his feet and tugged at Alice's arm.

"We might have known. One more blessing in an already miserable day," Viv lamented. She took a final bit of banana before dashing behind the nearest tree. They swiftly relinquished the tree to a billion biting ants, moving hurriedly back into the drenching rain. They gently stamped their bruised feet on the rocky ground.

The Datu scanned the gray skyline, then studied the novice hikers. "I know a shortcut back," he offered.

The shortcut followed a shallow, rocky riverbed, bypassing the house in the mountains where their shoes were waiting. They hobbled barefoot over the sharp rocks. Part-way back, they rested at a corn shelter near the river while the Datu sent guides to borrow horses. The travelers were another hour down the trail with the girls on horseback when Len's legs cramped severely. "Viv, would you mind if I rode awhile?" he asked in desperation.

Viv was still muffling her laughter as she walked behind

Len's horse when she heard dogs barking. She looked up and listened intently. Someone from the head of the line cried out, "We're home. There's Sinolon."

It was 10 P.M. Just ahead of them were a few scattered thatched houses and the lone dilapidated schoolhouse, shadowed by the darkness. "Well, it looks like a first-class hotel to me," Viv told the others.

"A mansion," Alice managed.

The trio bid their guides goodnight, then marched stiffly through the open door of the school. Viv lit the only candle on the table before the three of them collapsed on the stools that Len had made. One by one they began to laugh. They laughed with relief and at their own foolishness and frailty.

Before going to bed they huddled together and soaked their feet in pails of warm water, disinfecting them with merthiolate. Len sat between Viv and Alice, his trouser legs rolled to the knees, wiggling his red, inflamed toes in the water as he munched a stale sandwich.

"And I came to the field just to nurse sick Indians," Viv said as she added more hot water to the pails.

"But what a picnic," one of them exclaimed, "a billion ants and all."

"Very hitok," came the response.

"And medel," Viv added.

The others agreed. It was the kind of picnic they wouldn't want to write up in their monthly work report to the SIL director—not after their jungle-camp training. They had just broken every rule of survival. But at least the rookie recruits had begun to learn the language.

The next morning, in spite of his painful feet, Len was busy in his building program. By lunchtime a Tboli carrier arrived at the schoolhouse with three pairs of shoes. On Saturday the swelling in Len's feet was down enough for him to wear his tennis shoes home. He was hardly limping when he left Sinolon.

5
ALL THIS—
AND CHILDREN TOO

By the end of the girls' third week in the barrio, a whole stalk of bananas swung from one beam, coconuts from another; Tboli baskets full of fresh corn hung on poles. Stalks of sugarcane leaned against the wall. A little red hen was tied to the end of the house. And an orchid just ready to blossom swayed in the open window. All this had been given in exchange for medicine.

The very first patient to come for medicine stood in the open doorway with the little red hen tucked under one arm. "Na, friends," she greeted. The bracelets around her wrists and ankles pressed against scaly, excoriated skin.

After running her fingertips over the thick, raw areas, Viv sorted through medicine bottles. Choosing a bottle of white crystal powder, she mixed it with alcohol and spread the clear liquid over the woman's inflamed arms. The old woman smiled. As she took the container of medicine, she placed the hen in Vivian's hands. "I'm going now," she said. She went quickly, quietly down the porch steps, clutching the medicine bottle, the large, colorful combs in the back of her hair bobbing as she walked.

Several days later, the girls untied the hen from the corner post. The hen circled the post before discovering her freedom, then she followed them around like a pet. That evening as Alice said the supper blessing, there was a contented cluck, cluck and the flutter of wings in the middle of her prayer. Viv sneaked one eye open, then stifled a chuckle. The chicken was perched on Alice's head, obviously waiting for dinner.

The missionaries' business for the King those days was language study, six to eight hours a day, sometimes more. They were discovering that language was a wider barrier between people than an ocean. Viv and Alice had been at language learning three weeks when a man stood in their doorway and asked, "How long will it be before you have books in Tboli?"

From the same open doorway they could see the framework of the house the men were building for them.

"Friendship is worth more than money," the Datu said, and six weeks after Viv and Alice arrived in Sinolon, the house was sold at minimal cost to the translators. The new house was nice and shiny, sturdy and solid. It had a cogongrass roof, double layer bamboo walls, and split bamboo flooring. And it stood on stilts eight feet off the ground.

Now Datu Edwards had a thousand mountain people and two Melikan Bukay—white Americans—under his authority. He faced the responsibility in a cultural way by bringing a happy, bubbly, eleven-year-old orphan girl to live with the translators.

Viv and Alice hadn't planned on having children in their home. It was the Datu's suggestion, and it was a decision that would affect their entire ministry in Sinolon.

Viv looked at Bagong. Straggly strands of black hair cut across the child's smile. A worn Tboli blouse covered her thin arms.

"And so we have a family," Viv wrote in her monthly Wycliffe report. "Bagong can't speak a word of English except for a few memorized phrases she learned at the barrio school, but we're getting along just beautifully."

Shy, seven-year-old Gumbay came next, clean and neat, prim and proper, as different from Bagong as a gentle hill differs from a rugged mountain. Sumbwet, their fourteen-year-old language helper, also needed to belong to someone. And so Sumbwet moved in, too.

"What are we going to call you?" Sumbwet asked the translators soon after moving into the house.

"Oh, just call us by our names," they answered.

"Oh, no. To say a person's name—an older person's name—we couldn't do that."

"What then?" Viv asked.

"Would it be okay to call you mother?" he asked timidly.

Viv swallowed a chuckle. Being single, she hadn't planned on that. She continued to eye Sumbwet seriously.

"My people say sister, uncle, grandmother," he explained. He smiled. "We will call you Ye' Bong—Big Mother," he told Alice. Then, studying Viv, who tipped the scale lightly, he said, "You will be Ye' Udi—Little Mother."

Tado, the wildest boy in the neighborhood, wanted to live with the translators, too. "Try me. Try me," he begged.

"I believe the Melikan Bukay will tame my boy," the father said in response. So Tado came for a few months, violent temper and all, as the fourth of a growing family of children. He turned out to be a dandy language helper and more faithful than Sumbwet.

"The children are tremendous company and oh, the language practice," Viv wrote in a letter home. "They are so patient when Alice and I say, 'Repeat that word, please.' And the odd jobs they do! Sweeping under the house at sunup. Carrying pails of water on their heads. Washing the clothes down at the river, wrapping themselves in sheets and rushing against the current to rinse them. Gathering the wood. Doing the cooking. Alice and I couldn't do it alone."

In October the new Tboli family sat around the table,

close by the light of the Aladdin lamp that Gram and
Gramps had given Viv. They pored over a Northrup King
seed catalog, the children carefully making their selections.

"Carrots and cucumbers," Sumbwet said decisively.

"Onions," Tado added.

"Squash." Bagong was emphatic.

"How about some tomatoes?" Alice suggested. Viv
marked off the selection.

Gumbay hadn't said a word until she saw the picture of
the watermelon. She squealed with delight.

"Do you want to plant some watermelon?" Viv asked.

Gumbay's dark eyes sparkeled up at Viv. She nodded
shyly.

When the packages arrived from the States, the children
eagerly planted their seeds. Day after day they squatted in
front of their garden rows, digging and picking, watching for
the seeds to break ground. Finally the first seed sprouted.
"They're growing, Little Mother," Gumbay exclaimed.

Vivian grinned. She knew that it was for this work, this
place, and these people that the Lord had been preparing
her. The brown-eyed, black-haired children that called her
Ye' Udi were filling her days and thoughts and prayers. They
made the house in the Alah Valley home for her.

6

BREAKING PATTERNS
OF THE PAST

One Friday morning as Viv and Alice worked on language learning, Sumbwet looked puzzled. He frowned. "Very crooked, not following the tune, your Tboli words," he said sadly.

It made the girls dig even harder to learn the rhythm of Tboli. They needed to know the language before they would ever know the people. Scattered over the mountains beyond the Sinolon and hidden from view were small groups of Tboli homes, perched on the sides of steep hills. Tucked away in those homes along the mountain trails were people with cultural patterns that Viv and Alice were only beginning to understand.

With no twilight in Sinolon and having completed long, tedious hours of study, Viv and Alice retired early that Friday night. Without bothering to light the pressure lantern, they snuggled safely under their mosquito nets and were soon asleep.

The next morning they were up at the crack of dawn, their usual rising time, especially on market day. As the girls finished breakfast, people came from the market to the bamboo house for medicine, some just to visit. The men arrived in their abaca pants, wearing conical hats of woven bamboo reeds, with a glass knob at the tip. Many of the men had ridden horseback for hours to get there. Others had walked barefoot over the hills. Their women came behind them, balancing bundles of vegetables on the rolled towels on their heads, carrying bare-bottomed babies on their backs.

"Motuni we—come up, friend," Viv said. A tiny woman in a hand-embroidered blouse and colorful skirt came gracefully up the steps, her ankle bracelets clinking as she moved. The porch was already full of people sitting on the crude bamboo benches. The woman walked the length of the railing to the end of the porch. As she turned Viv could see the jagged bangs hanging low on her forehead; the familiar Tboli hair roll, the tuku, long and jet-black, was knotted artistically in the back. Large circular earrings dangled from both earlobes; they flashed in the sun as she gazed down at Gebung.

"Sick?" the woman questioned. Her eyes were harsh as she studied the young man. He lay on the porch, a thin blanket pulled up to his chin.

"He's sick, grandmother," Viv answered.

"The fever?"

Viv nodded. The boy couldn't be more than nineteen, if that, Viv thought. He had come to them late the night before, complaining of a festering wound and vomiting blood. All around him now, the people clicked their tongues about his sickness, saying, "Gebung is going to die."

The woman stared hard at Gebung. "He must call on the spirits to save him," she said.

Viv opened her mouth to protest, then stopped. She ached inside for the boy and the people. How frequently already she and Alice were confronted with pagan worship. Viv knew that only God could heal the boy, but she still did not have the Tboli words to tell the people.

In Tboli land Viv found many things new and different. There were no names for the days of the week. Sunday was just another day for Sumbwet to work for the Datu, stripping fiber from the abaca stalks with his bare hands.

Viv watched Sumbwet from the open window. His muscular back glistened in the sun as he helped the men hang the abaca fibers on the rocks to dry. Closer by, Gumbay and Bagong pounded the husks from rice, beating out a syncopated rhythm as their heavy pestles hit the hollowed log. Viv marveled at their boundless energy. Before the morning was over they would winnow the rice in large, flat baskets without spilling a kernel.

She turned back to the table, to the language work at hand. Alice had waited quietly for her. "You look troubled," she said to Viv.

"I was watching the children being caught up in a way of life so important to Tboli survival. I keep wondering how long it will be, what it will cost, before Sunday has a name—before it means something to the children." She shrugged, searching now for words in English. It wasn't just the days of the week that troubled her. She wanted these children, and the Tboli people, to know the Savior.

One custom would affect the Sinolon household more deeply than all the others. Less than a year after reaching Sinolon, Viv and Alice sat on the floor of the Datu's house with the chief elders, discussing the marriage dowry for Bagong.

"If Datu Edwards and Bagong's two brothers and her uncle ask for horses, Tboli blankets, and a number of agong-brass drums, the bridegroom will be in debt the rest of his life," Viv murmured.

Alice nodded. "It will take him a lifetime to pay back what he borrows to earn Bagong."

The elder lifted his hand for silence, quieting the roomful of people, allowing Kwel to speak for himself. Kwel sat in the center of the circle. All around him the elders reclined in various positions on the floor, spitting betelnut juice through bamboo slats. In the presence of that august assembly, the young bridegroom spoke up. "No matter what will befall us or our children, I will never leave Bagong."

Bagong was properly shy, scrutinizing her big toe while the elders pressed her for promises. "Do you want to marry Kwel?"

"Ah." Her answer was barely audible.

"Do you promise never to leave him even if you become thin and your clothes are ragged and your children sickly?"

"Ah," she repeated, the big toe of her right foot wiggling nervously.

Kwel waited, his dark eyes moving questioningly from one elder to the other. He stole a quick glance toward his intended bride, his boyish face serious, pleading. Bagong avoided his gaze, keeping her hands folded tightly in her lap. Earrings and two locks of hair framed her light brown face.

Viv smiled reassuringly at Kwel. He turned away, obviously embarrassed.

The Datu's decision finally came. "Kwel must have a house for himself and his bride complete with ladder, floor, walls, and a roof before the wedding can take place." In addition, the Datu, Bagong's brothers, and Viv and Alice would share two big horses as part of Bagong's dowry.

As they left the Datu's house, Viv and Alice felt disappointed, heavyhearted in the realization that now Bagong would not be going back to the barrio school. They felt helpless to combat childhood marriage contracts—all for the sake of a good bridal price. But there would be advantages in having a son-in-law. It wasn't Tboli custom to leave the parents. Kwel would stay nearby, providing food and firewood and working in the fields. That meant that Bagong would still be living near them, perhaps eager as always to read the stories they were translating.

Viv and Alice had given little thought to having other children in the home. But unknown to them, long before Bagong married, God was already preparing mountain-boy replacements for the house at Sinolon.

In the past when Datu Edwards wanted Tboli children to go to school, he sent policemen into the mountains to look for school-age boys. Before the policemen could reach the villages, parents would wrap food in banana leaves and push their children off to the woods, saying, "Run and hide. Don't come back until dark."

"They might harm you down at the barrio school," Selanting's father had explained to his son. "And I don't want them to hurt my child."

"But cousin Walan can sing songs and count to one-hundred," Selanting told his father.

Selanting's father smiled sadly. "Walan went off to the barrio school without a word to his parents. When he came back to the mountains, he was filled with new ideas."

Unlike his father, Selanting liked those new ideas. Walan had told him, "You ought to study, too. Then you and Mai will be learning something. Then you will become teachers."

As he stood before his father now, Selanting thought, *Good if my father would let me study, too.*

The morning Selanting finally started off to school, his mother cried. To make sure her son would learn well, she found a vine that clung tightly to the tree and rubbed it on his lips, cheeks, and forehead. "As the vine follows the tree, so may you, my son, follow that which is taught," she told him.

Then Selanting turned away and joined his three cousins—Walan, Mai, and Yadan. Leaving their mountain homes was hard, but going to school on the plains was harder. The lowlanders' children mocked the mountain boys, laughing at their long hair and baggy abaca trousers. "Bad the people from the mountains—just poor dirty folk," they said.

Selanting and his companions had no combs or changes of clothing. At night they slept under scratchy blankets

made from salt sacks. They had little food, and they didn't
have paper or pencils like the lowlanders. Nor could the
Tboli children understand what the teachers said in their
accented Filipino English or their Tagalog. Nevertheless,
four frustrated little boys stubbornly went back to the barrio
school again with each new school year.

After Selanting had finished his second year of school,
reports spread into the mountains about Viv and Alice.
"There are some white Americans living below now. Tboli
children are living with them and attending school," came
the report. "And the Americans' custom toward our people
is good."

"Let's go live with them," Mai suggested impulsively.

"Let's wait until market day; then let's go," Selanting
responded shyly.

After days of deliberation, and without saying a word to
Walan, the three third-graders went down the mountain trail
on market day to visit the Melikan Bukay.

The "white Americans" were still eating their noon meal
when the boys reached their front steps. For some time Viv
and Alice had been praying for girls to replace Bagong and
Gumbay, who had both married. But they had not prayed
for the trio of boys that faced them now.

"Na, friends," the boys greeted.

"Motun ye—come up, friends," Alice and Viv invited.

Yadan, the oldest one, was the spokesman. "We've come
to stay at your house and go to school and learn to read," he
annouced.

Viv chuckled. "You have?"

"Ah," Yadan nodded.

"It's true we are looking for someone to stay at our
house," Alice answered slowly, "but we're looking for little
girls." Little *girls,* she repeated to herself.

"That's all right," Yadan assured Alice. "You can have
little girls, too."

The two Americans searched frantically for words, trying to convey to their small guests that the plan was a poor one, even an impossible one.

Yadan shifted his weight to his other leg. "We will study hard," he promised.

Viv scrutinized the children. Yadan stood his ground boldly. Mai watched, his gaze intense, expectant. Selanting hid behind the others, unsmiling, almost frightened. Each boy had an extra pair of short trousers tucked under his arm. Viv hated to disappoint them, but she and Alice were not in Sinolon to raise a family. "We're on our way to visit a sick friend, to give an injection," Viv told the trio. "We really have to go now."

She expected them to be polite, to be cultural, to answer, "Oh, we are leaving, too." That would be good-bye, the end of it.

But Yudan said quietly, "We will just wait until you come back. You can give us your answer when you return."

As the translators walked down the trail, three little boys sat on their doorstep, eating Alice's homemade bread.

"I'm beginning to think three little boys sound appealing," Alice murmured, half to herself. Aloud she suggested, "Should we talk with the Datu on the way home?"

Viv wasn't sure she wanted to ask the Datu. She was afraid of his answer.

"Yes, they are good boys," Ma Flidu told them a short time later. "They worked well for the Ilocano lowlanders. They can carry water and wood, plant gardens and help do the weeding. *And they know the language.*"

That did it. Viv liked the idea.

Supper that night provided the first chance Alice and Viv had to really take a look at their new family. Across the table sat three shaggy boys steeped in the Tboli culture—boys who had broken the pattern of the mountain people by coming down the trail to Sinolon to study. They were good-looking, with black hair, brown eyes, quick smiles, and beautiful brown skin.

Viv noticed something else. Each boy had shiny round scars on his left arm, starting at the elbow and running in a straight line to the wrist. She cringed, knowing that those scars had been made by dipping little balls of kapok into coconut oil, placing them on the arm, and setting the kapok on fire. It was part of the pagan worship. The larger and deeper the scar, the brighter the light to frighten the evil spirits. The Tboli believed those scars would offer security in the next world when they crossed the swinging bridge into death.

But Viv quickly forgot the scars. Two of the youngsters, full brothers—Yadan on the right and Mai on the left—were speaking at once, "We'll teach you the Tboli words for everything."

"Ken," Mai giggled as he pointed to the rice.

"Tamban," Yadan informed them as he took a bit of dried fish.

But Selanting, the one sitting in the middle, was shy, reticent. He hardly said a word.

As Viv finished eating and looked at the three youngsters across from her, she wasn't thinking about the culture of the people or the cost of the Tboli New Testament. She was too excited, wondering if these little boys might be the ones that God would use to reach the mountain people.

7

MOUNTAIN SURVEY
TO A MAN NAMED DOMING

Across the Alah Valley, a day's journey from Sinolon by horseback, was a large lake that President Magsaysay had set aside for a national park. Northwest of Lake Sebu, on a mountain range that reached down to the sea, lived another group of isolated people.

Whenever Viv or Alice asked, "Who lives on those mountains?" the Tboli answered emphatically, "Manobos."

SIL Branch Director Dick Pittman wanted to allocate a new translation team among the Manobo people. In January 1955 he asked translators from three different language groups to climb that mountain range in search of Manobo.

The three translators—Bus Dawson, Myra Lou Barnard, and Vivian—made arrangements for guides and horses as far as Lake Sebu.

Bus encouraged the girls to pack lightly. "Take plenty of bath soap," he advised, but he strongly vetoed shampoo as a needless luxury. "A cake of soap and a stream will do," he told them.

Out went the shampoo. In went packets of powdered milk, dried fruits, and soup.

When Bus spotted deflated air mattresses tied for packing, he frowned. "We could get along without those," he teased.

Viv shook her head. "Maybe you can—I can't."

They set out on horseback at an easy pace, the girls in long-sleeved blouses and wide-brimmed hats, their feet in rusty stirrups.

Bus rode ahead of them in his Marine fatigues, a T-shirt, and old military boots. They rode over trails shaded by trees and cogon grass. Patches of sun peeked through, streaking their faces with sunburn. The trail rose slowly, steadily over slippery rocks and through tangled underbrush.

"My sunglasses," Myra Lou exclaimed suddenly. "I mean Jan's glasses. I borrowed them. They're gone."

Bus slipped off his horse and walked back, covering the thick trail with sweeping glances. "I can't find them." He ran his hand over his crew cut. "How'd you lose them, anyway?"

"Isn't it good trail procedure to close one's eyes and duck when going through overhanging bamboo?" Myra Lou asked, her voice thick with an Oklahoma accent.

Hours later, when they reached Lake Sebu, they found it lying like a long, narrow mirror between two mountain ranges. Their guides left them at the lake, flatly refusing to continue the journey into Manobo country. With only a vague plan for reaching the Manobo, the trio set out again the next morning with new guides.

They traveled on foot, climbing up one side of the mountain, sliding down the other. Crossing rivers. Wading up mountain streams. Brushing off ants, pulling off leeches. At the top of one steep incline one of the trio asked, "Where are Dick Pittman's Manobos?"

"I'll tell you one thing," Viv answered. "Everyone we've met so far is pure Tboli."

In those first few days of their trip they met Datu Dawata, sitting on a stump in a small clearing on the edge of the trail. Long, black hair hung loosely around his shoulders, a choker of beads circled his neck, and earrings covered his ear lobes. He sat stoically, combing his hair over his hand, ignoring the strangers on horseback.

Viv greeted him in Tboli. He ignored her completely, turning instead to Pedro, the guide, for information. The trio waited hopefully, silently, as Pedro pled on their behalf for clearance to continue the journey.

Finally the Datu stood. "Take them to my house," he told Pedro. "They will stay with me for three days. Then I will go with them to the house of my Manobo wife."

The next three days were spent at the Datu's crowded home. As the people gathered, the Datu shook his head solemnly. Then he pointed to Bus. "The white man carries no knife or gun—yet he started out, not knowing the way or the people."

But the color of their skin was not important once the Datu found that they would eat the native foods. "Do you eat yams? Cassava? Monkey? Rats?" In his contentment, he joined his fingertips and said, "Then we are the same. Brothers and sisters."

Later that same night the Datu asked, "Do you have medicine?"

Viv studied his skin, his eyes, the perspiration that dotted his upper lip. Could he be suffering from malaria? She placed two yellow tablets and one white one in his hand. He looked at them. "What is the work of the white tablet?" he asked. Viv told him.

"And the yellow one?" Again she used the Tboli she knew and explained its value.

"Do I chew them or swallow them? Do these tablets have 'enemies'—foods I cannot eat while taking them?"

Reassured, the Datu placed the three pills on the back of his tongue and with the entire household watching, swallowed. The people gathered closer to Vivian. "Does your basket have medicine for pinkeye?" asked one.

"For goiters?" asked another.

"For diarrhea?" a young mother questioned.

That first night, everyone sat around the fire in the middle of the bamboo floor, eating roasted yams. The surveyors made word lists, the flames from the fire providing their only light. They penciled the sounds on paper, carefully noting dialectical differences.

As the flames leaped up, the Tboli recounted the day's events: what happened in the house on the opposite mountain, the sickness of an old man nearby, the arrival of the strangers who were seaching for Manobo. The older men sang the stories of their people to the accompaniment of the bamboo guitar with its sad melodious tones. Outside, the croaking of tree frogs and the persistent chirp of crickets added their own discord. Then it was the translators turn to entertain. They put away their word lists and taught the people a hymn in Tboli. Falteringly, the people followed, word by word, line by line.

At the end of the song Viv asked, "Do you know this Jesus we're singing about?"

The Tboli shook their heads. "That name is new to our ears," the Datu told her.

Pedro, the guide who had remained for the night, said softly, convincingly, "If we were acquainted with God, we would follow his way. All of us in the mountains would."

Vivian nodded, misty-eyed. The survey in the mountains was making her keenly aware that there were hundreds more Tboli than she and Alice had ever dreamed. Their work of Bible translation was not limited to the Alah Valley.

Before retiring, Bus's compass was passed around the room for inspection; his ticking watch went from ear to ear. One old man, looking through Vivian's camera, spotted Bus through the lens. He turned to the man sitting beside him and said, "I see the white man's companion."

But of all the intriguing paraphernalia, nothing fascinated the people more than the air mattresses. As the trio sat puffing away, inflating their sleeping mats, the Datu approached cautiously. "Igam nawa—the mat of breath," he declared. Convinced that it would not explode, he eased himself to the corner of the air mattress. It took some urging before he reluctantly left his triumphant perch in the center of the mattress for his own straw mat in the corner of the house.

On the third afternoon, Bus jumped back and forth over a stick he held in his hands. "I've got to keep in shape," he explained to Viv and Myra Lou. "I won't be able to walk the trails tomorrow if I don't."

The crowd that gathered watched in amazement. Soon the young men untied their bolos and began to jump over them, mimicking Bus. Their earrings and long, black, knotted hair bounced rhythmically as they learned other school-day gymnastics. "More. More," they demanded.

Soon the men in the village were standing on their heads, spinning cartwheels, doing high jumps. The women on the sidelines clucked their tongues in admiration. Three fat little puppies barked at the excitement. Without thinking, Myra Lou impulsively barked back, mimicking the dogs.

As they prepared to leave the home of Datu Dawata early the next morning, the translators offered a gift to their host, setting the pattern they would follow on the entire trip. They showed him needles, safety pins, combs, matches. He frowned, obviously dissatisfied.

"How about powdered milk and a can of sardines?" Viv suggested.

"Or soap or salt?" Bus offered.

Again Datu Dawata frowned. Then he walked over to Viv's medicine basket and, with an authority all his own, selected two yellow tablets and one white one.

As they left him, Datu Dawata promised again, "I will meet you two days down the trail. Then I will take you to my Manobo wife." It was a promise he would be unable to keep.

The trio had given little thought to the mountain communication system—calling from mountain to mountain—but the story of Bus's gymnastics and Myra Lou's bark preceded them. No matter that Bus had tramped all day carrying a backpack; when he reached a new village the people would say, "We exercise now." And even if Myra Lou's voice appeared hoarse, they wanted her to bark. There were always people waiting to see them. The one who could jump over sticks. The one who could bark like a dog. And the one who could speak Tboli.

Toward the end of their three-week journey, when they were down to black coffee and vitamins, they found the nomadic Manobo living close to the sea. As the trio climbed the notched pole into the first Manobo home near a wild-pig trap, Viv ventured words of greeting in Tboli.

One man turned to the others in the home and, answering in Tboli, said, "Here is a woman who can speak our language."

Bewildered, Viv asked, "Are there no Manobo in this house?"

"Yes," said Malantaw Fanku, climbing over the railing, "My mother and my wife are Manobo." He pointed his chin at his wife, Asiyang, who stood shyly beside him. Then he added, "My in-laws, they are Manobo, too."

The trio swept out their notebooks. Would the Manobo words be like Vivian's Tboli? Or Bus's Kalagan? Or Myra Lou's Mandayan? It was soon evident that Malantaw and Asiyang were eager to help them learn. When they had difficulty determining a vowel sound, the Manobo couple removed the red quids of chewing mixture from their gums. They repeated the words slowly for the translators and then promptly popped the betelnut back into their mouths.

The next morning, when the missionaries reached the Sungen River, Malantaw said, "From here on all the houses are Manobo."

The Manobo homes, with walls of tree bark and roofs of rattan leaves, teetered high off the ground. The people had practically no possessions, but the elders were eager to have someone come to study their language, to have books in their own dialect, and to have their children learn to read.

When Bus, Myra Lou, and Viv reached the coast at the end of their survey, the guides pointed back to clusters of Manobo homes on the mountainsides, each cluster a possible place for allocating a new translation team. The guides would head home the next morning, while the three surveyors would gladly return to Sinolon by way of the sea. But God had one more special blessing. A small group of Tboli believers lived on the coast.

Twenty years before, along the same southern seacoast, a Christian and Missionary Alliance worker had stopped his launch to hold meetings with the Tboli. The missionary talked about God, about God's Book—what it said about sin. What it said about the Lord Jesus dying for them. In one of those areas a chief and his entire family, including his seven-year-old son, Doming, came to trust the Lord. There was little additional training except the occasional visits from the missionary, but the tiny group remained true to God.

When Doming, a grown man now, met the Bible translators, he said, "My father dreamed many years before that someday, someone would come to teach our people God's Word. Now I see the answer to his dream. If you come back," Doming told Vivian, "I will help you put our words on paper."

At rice-planting time in the spring of that year, Vivian and Alice went back to the coast where the Manobo survey had ended to spend time with Doming and his father, Datu Saplon. Datu Saplon's home, a house without walls, was old, sagging on high stilts under the coconut palms. The shaggy grass roof was patched, the split bamboo flooring broken in places. Doming and his neighbors were working in their rice fields. But true to his promise, even when his neighbors laughed at him, Doming left the fields to help the girls plunge into initial translation.

They sat around a crude kitchen table, fighting off mosquitoes, working long into the evening hours, stopping only twice a day for a meal of rice and vegetables. The table was covered with books, notepads, paper, and a typewriter. In the middle of their work, Doming paused and rested his bony elbows on the table. "Working in the fields is much easier," he declared.

When the people passed by the house, Doming called out to them, "You come. You stop. Look into these words. They aren't Ilocano words or English words. They are your own Tboli words. You can understand them."

As Viv and Alice translated verses on heaven and the home God was preparing for his people, Doming said, "When the old folk hear these beautiful words, they will cry."

At the end of the translators' three-week visit, other visitors from back in the mountains stopped to spend the night. The old house under the coconut palms was dark, the floor covered with straw sleeping mats. The only sound was Doming quietly telling the guests what God's Word said, his voice tender with understanding as he answered their questions.

In the early hours of the morning one man woke his wife. He shook her firmly. The woman sat up, alarmed, alert. "You must hear Doming talk," her husband whispered.

Viv lay on her own straw mat, listening to Doming, thinking how shallow her own devotion was in comparison. "Oh, God, how I want to be able to understand every word," she prayed. "I want to be able to speak Tboli well. I want to know the ways of these people well enough to think the same way, reason the same way."

During their last moments in Datu Saplon's little settlement, Doming's father gripped each girl's hand quickly, briefly. "For hundreds of years the Tboli lived in these mountains. But my generation was the first to be told about Jesus. . . ." He stopped, the thought obviously overwhelming him. "And to think we might have missed it also." He shook his head, burying his big bare toe in the sandy beach.

Viv and Alice turned away hurriedly. When they were almost out of sight, Doming's grandfather called to them. "'Will you come back?" he asked wistfully. "Will you come back?"

Several days later, on 18 June 1955 at seven o'clock in the morning, Viv and Alice were flying over the mountains of Mindanao—temporarily leaving the Tboli people—on their way to a year's group assignment in Manila.

8
MYRA LOU: ROOM 401

The next time Myra Lou Barnard and Vivian Forsberg met, Myra Lou was burned from the edge of her hairline to the tips of her toes.

Myra and her partner, Jan, had been visiting in the home of friends at the Baptist Clinic in Malaybalay, an hour from Nasuli, when a brand-new kerosene refrigerator caught fire. In attempting to smother the flames with potholders, Myra Lou caught the explosion full force.

In seconds the entire room was in flames, the ceiling scorched, the floor burning. The word "fire" ran through the mission compound.

News of the accident reached Manila the following morning in a crisply worded telegram. A second telegram followed a few days later: "Can Vivian Forsberg come? We need nurses, plasma, medicine."

Viv was flown in at once to help care for Myra Lou. When she arrived at the clinic at Malaybalay and walked into Myra Lou's room, she was shocked. Her own skin turned clammy, the hair on her arms prickled. Myra was wrapped in bandages, her face brown and crispy, her thick, dark hair singed, her body covered with second- and third-degree burns. Only the squint lines around Myra's eyes were untouched by the fire.

Viv managed a smile, her stomach muscles knotting. "Hi, Myra," she said softly.

Myra's eyes moved slightly. "They tell me my condition is good," she told Viv, "but I feel rotten."

Vivian relaxed a little. Myra's voice was the same, her humor still there.

On a Sunday weeks after the accident, Vivian accompanied Myra Lou and Jan in the Philippine Air Force flight from Malaybalay to Manila. As Myra Lou's stretcher was placed gently on the floor of the plane, Dr. Linc Nelson and the rest of the folks from the Baptist compound huddled around her, singing "He leadeth me."

When they finished singing, Jan and Viv eased into the parachuters' metal seats that lined both sides of the plane. They were silent, apprehensive as they fastened their safety belts. Viv was praying, frightened at the thought of not having Dr. Nelson on hand for the three-and-a-half-hour flight to Manila. She was even more concerned that they had no pain medicine on board. God reassured Viv, "I'm with you. Don't fear."

Less than an hour from Malaybalay, engine trouble delayed the plane in Cagayan de Oro. As they waited for repairs, Myra Lou became restless, feverish and air-hungry. Finally a Philippine Air Force officer came on board and introduced himself. "I'm a flight surgeon. Is there anything I can do to help?" he asked.

"Do you have anything for pain—any codeine?" Viv responded.

He did.

Hours later, back in flight and with daylight gone, cold settled in. They were flying high, without the benefit of a heater. Flashes of lightning streaked across the dark sky. One engine churned, roaring against the driving rain like a loose wheel on a Model T. The metal seat was cold against Viv's back. She gazed at her friend, who was shivering, dozing fitfully on the army stretcher in the aisle.

She reflected that it had been after their survey trip in the

mountains in search of Manobo that Myra did what few dare
do. Longing to be a more effective Christian, Myra had
asked the Lord to send a purifying fire into her life. Viv
looked away, avoiding Jan's questioning gaze. She swallowed hard at the lump in her throat, wondering how God
would use Myra's pain-wracked body to answer that prayer
for effectiveness.

It was 9:30 in the evening, thirteen and one-half hours
after they took off from Malaybalay, when the plane finally
touched down in Manila. SILers had an ambulance waiting.
With the wail of its siren clearing the way, it sped them
through the traffic of Manila to the American hospital. By
midnight Myra's temperature soared to 106 degrees. Viv sat
through the night in the quiet of room 401 with her finger
tips on Myra's pulse.

Three weeks after reaching Manila, Myra Lou was losing
more body fluids than she was retaining. Blood transfusions
were a steady diet. Contractures were of secondary concern; doctors were fighting for her life.

The Philippine branch of Bible translators was still young
and growing in number. But small points of friction had
crept in. For some, molehills had mushroomed; loneliness
gripped others. With Myra Lou's injury, these differences,
these petty irritations, quickly melted in the bonds of Christian love. The purifying fire that Myra Lou had asked for had
started in other hearts, too. For long months the branch was
keenly aware of the enormity of heaven, with Myra Lou
almost there.

"We are not alone in the battle for our colleague," Dick
Pittman reminded them. "Hundreds and hundreds of people—many of them total strangers—are writing and praying and giving, helping with the mounting hospital bills."

At the hospital, weeks began to revolve around Friday
nights, when Myra Lou was taken to surgery for debride-
ment and dressing changes. When all the bandages and

paddings were removed she was pitifully thin. The hard crusty skin was removed, leaving raw, oozing flesh. Myra Lou's cheerful spirit was contagious. She prayed for her nurses, saying, "God, give them courage for my dressing changes, even when I flinch with pain."

One Friday, weeks after reaching Manila, she said to Viv, "Don't feel sorry for me; the Lord didn't permit this, he planned it."

Before Myra Lou left for the operating room, Viv said encouragingly, "Pretty soon you'll be all new, inside and out."

Tears welled in Myra Lou's eyes. "Oh, Viv, I hope so." She especially wanted the newness inside.

Dr. Aenlle, one of the Filipino physicians assigned to Myra Lou, had finally sorted out the nurses who cared for her. If he wanted a pessimistic report he asked for the nurse from Canada. "If I want the situation as it really is, I go to Miss McKay," he explained. "But if I want an optimistic report, I go to Miss Forsberg."

The hundreds of people praying for Myra Lou were praying for her nurses, too. In February, six months after Myra Lou's injury, Vivian went through a period of rebellion. Again and again as she walked into room 401, the stench from Myra Lou's burns, her own discouragement, and the longing to get back to Sinolon and the Tboli plagued her.

At times as she hurried down the steep front steps of the Wycliffe group house and pushed through the front gate to catch the jeepney, she cried out silently, "Oh, God, I just can't stand the next twelve hours of pain and duties and smells. I can't stand watching Myra Lou go from one moment of agony to another."

Vivian hated herself for her own rebellion. She could hardly pray, knowing that Myra Lou knew how hard it was to leave the translation work; Myra Lou had left one herself.

It was during those times of heaviness within that Viv

again asked the Lord to live out his life through her, to really be her Lord and Master. To fill her with love, joy, peace, kindness, gentleness. In God's own special way, he was saying to her, "Enlarge the place of thy tent . . . spare not, lengthen thy cords, and strengthen thy stakes."

The enlargement was personal this time. She had to lengthen the cords of her own understanding, to strengthen the stakes of her own walk. It was as though he had spoken aloud to her, "If you can learn submission so well that it becomes a habit with you, then these months with Myra Lou will be the most valuable months of your life." He was reminding her that without obedience there could never be a Tboli New Testament. Another New Testament was at stake, too—the one that Myra Lou and Jan wanted to finish.

Months later, as SIL cleared Myra Lou's documents for leaving the country, Dick Pittman asked for a reentry permit for her.

"Is she coming back?" asked the astonished official.

"She's coming back," was the affirmative reply.

Saturday, 20 October 1956, fourteen months after Myra Lou was burned, friends and hospital personnel crammed the lobby of the American hospital, watching the arrival of a large U.S. Air Force ambulance. Three Air Force officers stepped out, strode into the hospital, and quickly found their way to room 401. "Are you the patient going on the plane?" one of the men asked.

"I dunno. Am I?" Myra Lou teased.

"That's what it says here," the officer replied, tapping the paper in the palm of his hand.

"Well, when do we start?"

The officer grinned. "Is now soon enough?"

Several packed cars followed the ambulance to the international airport in Manila. Inside there were two patients: a twenty-seven-year-old polio victim in a portable respirator, and Myra Lou. The polio patient was going to a hospital in

Buffalo, New York. Myra Lou was on her way to Oklahoma City's Wesley Hospital, where she had taken her own nurse's training.

When they arrived at the airport, the wide cargo hatch of a U.S. Navy plane was open, the ramp in place. As they carried Myra Lou on board, once again her friends and colleagues sang "He leadeth me."

Viv watched tearfully as the door of the four-engine, Super Constellation shut her patient from view. Then the plane taxied down the runway and soared off, heading home to the States—an old war plane on an errand of mercy.

9
BACK TO SINOLON

As she sat in the Manila group house, curled comfortably on the rattan couch by the window, Viv was homesick. She had just read Selanting's hand-written Tboli note, "If you don't hurry back we won't be acquainted when you get here."

As she thought of Sinolon, the comforts of city living no longer mattered—sleeping on an innerspring mattress, reading by electricity, buying popsicles from the Magnolia man. Even a second invitation to her most memorable city event—the personal visit and interview with President Magsaysay—couldn't detain her now. What Viv wanted most was to get back to Sinolon, to language learning, back to the bamboo thicket where Alice and the Tboli were.

Weeks later, when she arrived at the barrio, Selanting was leaning out the window, grinning from ear to ear. Viv waved. Selanting shaded his eyes. "Who is this stranger?" he teased.

Under the house on bamboo stilts, Walan was sharpening his bolo, smiling shyly. But two of the younger boys ran down the steps to meet her, their eyes shining, as glad to see Viv as she was to see them. Her smile broadened.

"Welcome home," Alice said as they walked up the steps together.

Viv was still grinning. "It's good to be home—good to be surrounded by Tboli children."

That night Alice took the literacy materials from the shelf and spread them across the kitchen table. "People are coming for reading lessons all the time now," she said excitedly. "Imagine Tboli reading, really reading."

"I can hardly wait to hear them," Viv admitted.

"You've missed some other excitement," Alice went on. "You should have been here for the measles' epidemic. We could have used you. We gave so many injections . . . it seemed like everyone had chills and fever, bronchial complications, or dysentery." Alice rubbed her arms. "You can still see some of my blotches."

"You'll make a good nurse yet," Viv chuckled, but her expression sobered as Alice talked of the boys.

"Mai has run away again."

"He'll come back," Viv responded optimistically.

"I'm not so sure this time. He wants to get ahead. Do things on his own."

A minute passed and then Viv asked, "Is the land problem growing, too?"

"The squatters are claiming the Tboli fields—cutting down their abaca and bananas. Even the Tboli school. . . ."

"Aren't the people fighting back?" Viv asked.

Alice sighed with concern. "The Tboli try—there have been a few isolated skirmishes. But what can they do? The law seems to be on the side of the lowland settlers."

Viv frowned. It was obvious that it wasn't getting better. The Tboli were still being pushed back into the hills— harder to reach than ever.

Shortly after Viv returned, she and Alice entertained a distinguished guest from a neighboring town. Outside, the rainy season was in full motion, the large tropical droplets splattering through the thatched roof. As Viv talked with their guest, attempting to explain what two Melikan Bukay were doing in Tboli land, Alice pushed the furniture around the room to avoid the raindrops.

Finally the guest said in his accented English, "I see then that you are somewhat educators."

"No, they are not educators," Selanting quickly responded. "They are learners." It was true. They were learners of the language, learners of the culture, learners in making Christ known and loved among the Tboli, learners for the first five years on the field.

Now, as Alice and Viv prepared for their first furlough, they wondered what would happen to the boys in their home. These young men had sung hymns and heard the Bible stories, but they didn't really understand how dearly the man on the cross—the risen Savior—loved them. They didn't really know him. Much more language learning was necessary before the translators could clearly explain it to them.

God already had the answers. Four of the boys would leave their mountain homes to attend the Filipino Christian school on the seacoast near Doming's place. Attending chapel at Edenton was compulsory, and Bible study was part of the curriculum. But the girls didn't know this when they prayed. Nor did they know that the Christian and Missionary Alliance would send a worker into the area who would have a strong influence in the lives of the boys, especially on Mai.

Before sailing for the States, Viv accompanied the boys on the forty-five-mile trip to the seacoast. At Marbel, enroute to Edenton, Selanting said, "Would it be good, Little Mother, if Yadan, Manib, and I had another companion to study with us?"

"That would be very good," Viv replied. "Have you found one?"

Selanting smiled cunningly. "Mai is over at the bakery."

And Viv answered, "You run and talk with him, Ting. Good if Mai goes with you."

Selanting found Mai at the bakery, reading a comic book. "Would you like to study again, Mai?"

"Would I," Mai sighed wistfully. "If there were only someone to help."

"Come study with us on the coast. Our mothers want you to come."

Mai looked doubtful. He had left the household at Sinolon twice before, without a word of good-bye. "If only they would want me again," he answered pensively.

"They want you, if only you won't turn back."

"I won't anymore," Mai promised.

Later, when the four boys said good-bye to Viv at Edenton, Yadan asked, "What will you do on furlough in the big land?"

She thought a minute. "Speak . . . study."

"For a whole year?"

"Most of the time."

"Will you miss us?" Selanting asked shyly.

Viv smiled. She knew it would be a year of rest from pouring sulfa powder into deep ulcer sores, giving out pills for dysentery, putting ointment in infected eyes. But she would miss the brown-eyed children's swarming over the porch or underfoot every waking hour of the day, calling, "Ye' Bong, Ye' Udi."

"Yes, I'll miss you," she assured him.

"Will you come back?" Mai asked pointedly.

"We will," Viv promised. The jeepney was ready to go. She waved at the boys, thinking, "Oh, God. We have a stake in these lives. Will you strengthen them . . . will you keep them?"

As the vehicle took off, she waved again, then settled against the wooden seat, her thoughts mixed. Thoughts of the boys. Thoughts of furlough in the big land.

For most of her furlough, almost every letter from the boys ended, "Don't forget us. And hurry and come back."

That's what Viv and Alice intended; they would both return to the Tboli work. But that summer Alice spent eleven weeks on the SIL staff at the University of Oklahoma, where one of her students—a tall, quiet, dark-haired young man from New Jersey—seemed more serious about the instructor than he did about his studies.

The following winter, Alice boarded the *S.S. American Mail* at pier 88 in Seattle, Washington, for her return to the Philippines, a diamond on her finger.

Seven weeks later, in January 1959, Vivian boarded another freighter at the same pier, her three barrels in the hold of the ship packed solid. She was sailing back for her second term in the Philippines. They had left the warmth of Hawaii and set a steady course toward the Islands, moving through wintery seas. Viv sat on the open deck in a woolen jacket, her winter coat buttoned to the neck, a wool kerchief knotted under her chin, blankets wrapped around her legs. As she huddled there, she wondered, *If I have only one thing to ask and receive from you, Lord, for the next five years, what should I ask?*

At first she thought she wanted to know the language and the people more than anything. Or should she ask to be able to lead them to an understanding of forgiveness in Jesus? Perhaps she should ask for love or joy or peace. The more she thought about it, the more certain she was that she should ask for peace. *If I have peace with God and man,* she thought, *all other things will fall into place. But if I lose my peace with you, God, I might as well go home. I'd be no use to people, no good to anyone—out of sorts with myself and my fellowman.* And so she asked for peace.

When they reached Yokohama, Japan, on Friday morning at 9 A.M., Beatrice Long, Viv's roommate from nursing school, was on the dock, waiting for them. "How come you're so late?" she called up to Viv.

"Are we late?" Viv called back.

"Yes," Bea answered. "I've been here since Monday."

"When were we supposed to get here?" Viv asked innocently.

"Tuesday morning—early."

For the next forty-eight hours, Viv discovered a wintery Japan. They stayed in Tokyo, a city bulging with new construction. Bea spoke Japanese fluently as she guided Viv though the narrow streets into the small shops, where the people were padded for warmth. They ate with chopsticks, laughed and reminisced, and slept those two nights under eight thicknesses of woolen blankets.

As the ship pulled out of Yokohama Harbor two days later, Bea waving on the dock, seven United States destroyers and two aircraft carriers steamed past them on maneuvers. It was impressive—impressive enough for one of Viv's traveling companions to say, "Hey, get up The Stars and Stripes so they know which side we're on."

In Manila other friends were waiting when the ship docked, eager to help Viv in the reentry procedures. She was quickly processed through the government offices and soon was on her way south by interisland boat to Mindanao. But arrival at Nasuli was the real homecoming. Alice and the Dawsons were there to greet Vivian, and Myra Lou Barnard came across the lawn toward Viv, barely limping. As Viv watched Myra Lou come toward her, she remembered a little boy's prayer offered shortly after Myra Lou was burned: "Dear God, help Aunt Myra Lou stand on her feet so she can get out and see the world again."

Viv couldn't stop grinning. Myra Lou was standing and back in the translation work with Jan.

Viv and Alice were anxious to make a satisfactory reentry into their own translation project. In spite of the rumors that the Tboli were all living in the mountains, they found Datu Ma' Flidu living in the same house in Sinolon and old Siki and his family still living across the trail. The avocado seeds and the four-inch pine they had planted during first term were taller than the house. A neighbor's dog whimpered, wiggled, and yipped his welcome. Children, who were babies when the girls left, chattered happily with them. The old grandmother, one of the first women they had ever known in Sinolon, came over immediately—even thinner and more wrinkled than when they left. She hobbled into Alice's arms and cried.

But the biggest blessing of all was their family of boys. The man on the cross—the risen Savior—had become real to them. "It was God's Word we were studying at Edenton," Selanting explained. "Dared we disobey it?"

And for Mai, who had not gone back for the second term at Edenton, there had been a special change of events. While Viv and Alice were on furlough, the Christian and Missionary Alliance had established several teaching points among the Tboli. The new C&MA missionary had used Mai as her interpreter. As soon as he understood the truth, Mai set out for the mountains to tell others; Selanting's mother had been among the first in the mountains to believe in Jesus.

And these boys—the ones who remained at Edenton as well as Mai, Walan, and a boy named Gung—were learning to teach their own people, week by week. Viv marveled. These boys, these teen-agers, seemed so young in faith, so limited in knowledge. They seemed to know so little, believe so much. But they were fresh and sincere in their love and obedience.

The boys had one other suprise for Viv and Alice. They had chosen three of their little brothers—Bedung, Kasi, and Fludi—to live at the house at Sinolon.

"Then you won't be lonely," Mai explained. "While we're away at high school."

"And you will really learn the language," another suggested.

"It is the custom," Yadan said matter-of-factly.

The older boys would be going to high school at King's Institute, a Christian agricultural school in nearby Marbel. Shortly before leaving for King's Institute, the high schoolers came asking, "What was the day of my being born?"

As each child came to their home, the team had selected a birth date for him, basing it on Tboli seasons. The moon season for cutting down trees to make their rice fields; the season for planting; the season for weeding; and the season for harvesting rice. And after the rice was eaten, there was the season for being hungry, when the people survived completely on root crops.

For Mai, Yadan, and Selanting, the translators had asked the parents, "In what season was this child born? Was it at the beginning or end of that season? Were you cutting trees at the bottom of the mountains where you always begin? Or were you nearing the top and almost finsihed?" And so the team figured out as closely as they could what month and day each boy was born, carefully noting the date down in a book so they wouldn't forget.

They would do the same for Bedung, Kasi, and Fludi. The boys would need that date only once or twice in their lives—once when they entered the barrio school for the six years of elementary training, and again when they completed the sixth grade and entered the Filipino high-school system.

The night before the older boys left for Marbel, they all gathered around the kitchen table once more to read and discuss God's Word. Viv and Alice were pleasantly surprised, joyful, when Selanting said, "Will you translate my verse into Tboli?"

"Your verse?"

"Yes, this one . . . 'If I regard iniquity in my heart, the Lord will not hear me.'"

10
IN THE MIDDLE OF BEGINNINGS

Shortly after getting back from furlough, Vivian wrote her parents, "It's a wonderful thing to be in the middle of beginnings. Now Alice and I have a stake in many Tboli lives, but as our family of boys grows during this second term in the Philippines, so does our responsibility."

There were many firsts. The people were beginning to understand that God loved them. JAARS—the Jungle Aviation and Radio Service of Wycliffe—began service in the Philippines. The first Helio Courier, the *Spirit of Seattle*, arrived along with radio-receiver-transmitter sets for each translation team. Walan, the oldest of the boys, became the first Tboli high-school graduate. There was the first Tboli translator to be married; a first Tboli baptismal service. And there was the first Tboli in the Sinolon area to be "absent from the body, present with the Lord."

That was in April, not long after the girls returned to Sinolon. Two men from the mountains arrived in the late afternoon and quickly singled out Selanting, who was cooking vegetables at the fire table.

"Tomorrow you'd better go to the mountains and see your mother," one of them said.

"Why?" Ting asked.

"She's very sick."

Ting sat down on the steps with the men. "She's already dead, isn't she?" he asked softly.

73

"Yes," the older man answered. "Already dead."

With a grief that was fresh and searing, Selanting turned to Vivian and said, "My mother has died."

The man nodded again. "That's true. She left this morning when the sun climbed about half-way in the sky."

Days before, when Selanting last saw his mother, she had said, "I don't feel well, Ting." Viv and Alice had sent back malaria medicine for her fever and chills. They had heard no more until now.

Selanting's grief was mingled with fear. For centuries, the Tboli had maintained their traditional ways of life with little interest in the world beyond their borders. Now Ting asked, "Have my long periods of absence from the mountains angered the spirits? Is that why they have taken the soul of my mother?"

He wanted to shout at the men and deny that his mother had died, to cry out asking, "What will happen to my younger brothers and sisters?"

He couldn't face the thought of his mother placed in a coffin in a hollowed-out log. He didn't want to hear friends and relatives saying to his mother, "Why did you leave your husband and children and fields?"

Ting wanted to run back to school—to King's Institute— until it was all over. But Mai gently reminded him, "Your mother has arrived in heaven. Of all the people in the mountains, she listened to the stories from God's Word. She believed them. Would not this be an opportunity to tell the people of God's love? Is it not your responsibility to tell them?"

Grief was too fresh for Selanting to answer. It was still hard for him to understand that his mother had breathed her last breath here on earth and taken the next breath in heaven.

"Death for your mother will not mean loneliness and misery," Viv told him gently. She wanted to add that his mother had not crossed the slippery bridge of death alone; she was not groping in the darkness as her Tboli ancestors had. Vivian wanted to assure him that his mother had left her little nipa hut in the mountains and moved into a mansion. But the words wouldn't come. Nor was she free to slip an arm around Selanting's trembling shoulders; custom forced her to keep an appropriate distance.

Slowly the rest of the household at Sinolon gathered around Selanting to pray. The vegetables on the fire table were forgotten in their love for the boy who was hurting.

Ting was the last one to pray. In a broken voice he quietly told the Lord, with all the household at Sinolon listening, "Now that my mother can no longer tell her friends and relatives what faith in Jesus means, I will." And as he prayed he gave himself to God so that his own people could have God's Word and be taught God's way in their own language.

Before breakfast the next morning, Mai and Selanting were off to the mountains to share the message with mountain people. "Let not your heart be troubled . . . God shall wipe away all tears."

That evening two radiant, breathless boys returned. Mai was shiny with perspiration as he reached the top of the steps. "We told many about Jesus today, and their listening was beautiful. It is very easy to teach from God's Word when there is no sin in your body," he said.

Ting agreed.

From then on Ting began to translate God's Word in earnest, with infinite patience and the capacity to work all day without tiring. Many times after that the translators heard Selanting tell the Lord that he had not forgotten the promise he made on the night of his mother's death. "And if I ever forget, dear God," Ting prayed, "will you quickly remind me again?"

11

AT THE HOUSE
IN SINOLON

Alice Lindquist was beautiful in satin and lace when she married Kenneth Maryott, the fellow Bible translator who had been her student during furlough. Following Alice's marriage in Manila, sturdy, dark-haired Lillian Underwood, a graduate nurse, joined Vivian as the second "big mother" in the house at Sinolon.

Lillian, the oldest of eleven children, came from a farm twenty miles from Binghamton, New York. While listening to a radio program during her nurses' training days at Wilson Memorial Hospital in Johnstown City, she came to know Christ personally. Lil, with her own deep contagious chuckle, fit into the buzz around Sinolon as if she were born for it.

Shortly after she arrived, a beautiful sunset splashed across the late afternoon sky, shadowing itself in the mountains, leaving the viewers breathless before it slipped quietly into darkness. Viv smiled at Lil. "It looks as though the Lord just added his special blessing to our new partnership at Sinolon."

Lil soon discovered that the Gospel was already taking hold on individual lives, changing the boys at the house at Sinolon. When she met Fludi, the younger brother of Mai and Yadan, he was no longer a scrawny little runt dressed in an old shirt and torn pants, his chin barely reaching the tabletop. He had grown a smidgen. His face was fuller, his eyes sparkling as he sat beside Lil at the table, swinging his still-bony legs. "We'll teach you Tboli," he promised, carefully choosing his English words.

"I'd like that," said Lil. She paused, then added, "Is your home far away?"

"On the very top of the second mountain, three hours on the trail from Sinolon," he replied quickly, stuffing some rice in his mouth.

Viv dipped some rice on her own plate. "Everything Mai and Yadan learned from us they told Fludi. But Christianity meant nothing to him. Not until he learned that Christ could protect him from evil spirits."

Fludi agreed. "Then I listened. Then I learned to talk with God," he told Lil.

"But there was one thing he didn't do," Mai interrupted. "He didn't quit smoking."

Viv nodded, remembering. "Here in Tboli land, tobacco is raised with the vegetables. It's an important crop. Parents often give it as a gift."

Fludi went on with the story. "One day when I went to market with my father to sell abaca, he bought me three cigarettes. I stuck them in the waist of my pants and then, with my father's permission, I started down the hot, dusty trail a couple of kilometers to the house where Mai was staying. Mai was outside, all alone."

"I was weeding in the front yard when Fludi arrived," Mai said. "It was hot, so Fludi lifted the bottom of his shirt to wipe the perspiration off his face."

"It was too late when I remembered," Fludi admitted. "Mai had already spotted the three cigarettes tucked in my belt. I was so ashamed."

"What did Mai say?" Lil asked.

"Mai pulled me down beside him and said, 'If you are going to be a follower of God you have to keep your body clean.'"

"I went home that day, trudging up the mountains all by myself. My breath grew heavier and heavier. Before I got to the top of the second mountain, I stopped and thought about Mai's words. I pulled the three cigarettes from my belt, rolled them against the palm of my hand for a moment, and then tossed them down into the gully. The rest of the climb was easy," Fludi said, his eyes shining.

Lil looked around the table at the other boys. Selanting eyed her steadily, his handsome, bronzed face smiling in return. Viv had already warned Lil, "Selanting is a great one for finding kids who need a home and want to go to school."

Lil would keep her eye on Selanting. But it wasn't long before Selanting chose Gadu to come and live with them. He was only a little first-grader with big, brown eyes and long eyelashes—eyes that asked to be part of the family. He was bouncy like Peter Rabbit, enthusiastic about everything, and not at all troubled that he was already pledged to marry Selanting's sister.

But he had one problem, a major one. He had a tremendous penchant for lying.

Lil, who was practical and economical, fought Gadu's coming. There were already too many boys, too much responsibility. "Viv, don't you think we should wait?"

Viv shrugged her shoulders. "It's the custom," she offered lamely.

Several summers after Lil moved into the household, Fludi and Gadu decided to earn some money working for an Ilocano family. They had just finished building a pig fence. There was one stick of bamboo left over. Fludi and another young fellow began to play and tease, each grasping the remaining piece of bamboo.

"Here, Fludi, hit it hard enough so it will divide the bamboo," Sol challenged.

Fludi pulled out his bolo. Just as his long knife came down, Sol teasingly jerked the bamboo stick. The bolo slashed into Fludi's thumb, splitting the long bone down through the middle and knicking the second knuckle. Glaring angrily at Sol, Fludi lifted his bolo to strike again. Then, as if a hand had come down on his own, he put his bolo away.

"I'm going home," Fludi said quietly, as blood splattered from his wound.

Before Fludi and Gadu took off across the cornfields, the Ilocano farmer wrapped a rag around Fludi's loose thumb and tied a second rag like a tourniquet around his upper arm. Up a hill the boys scurried, then down to the river. When they reached the grove of trees near the river bank, Fludi's arm throbbed. He turned to Gadu and said, "Gadu, I'll never make it."

Gadu whirled around and whipped off his straw hat. He faced his friend. "Fludi, pray," Gadu begged.

Fludi's voice was barely a whisper. "Heavenly Father, help me make it the rest of the way home." Then the boys slipped down the bank to the water's edge. Gadu, small as he was, picked up his injured companion and carried him across the swiftly moving current.

Viv saw the boys coming up the bank toward the back steps, Fludi's thin, brown face as white as it could be.

"Oh, Little Mother, Fludi has been hurt," Gadu called. "His thumb is almost gone."

Lil held the door open as Gadu carried Fludi up the steps. She helped him stretch Fludi on the kitchen floor. He lay quietly, his flat nose covered with perspiration.

Viv trembled as she knelt down beside him. "Fludi, we'll look at the thumb. Maybe we can put it back on."

"It's almost all the way off, Little Mother," Gadu warned her.

The minute Viv loosened the tourniquet, blood squirted, soaking Fludi's T-shirt. The thumb was cut clear through. "That's the way it is," Fludi told them.

Lil was out the door immediately, heading for the C&MA missionary to borrow the only available vehicle for the trip to the doctor in Banga. After a dusty, exhausting journey to the doctor's and back, Viv tucked the sleeping net around Fludi. "I'm staying right here near you tonight," she said reassuringly. "If you wake up, call me. I'll get you a pain pill."

Hours later, in the middle of the night, Viv awakened in the darkness. Fludi was leaning over her. "Little Mother, Little Mother, are you all right? What's the matter?"

Viv sat up, dazed. "What's wrong, Fludi? Are you all right? Do you want a pill?"

"No. What's wrong with you? *You* were moaning, crying out in your sleep."

Viv grinned sheepishly. She had been dreaming about Fludi's thumb. "Just dreaming," she said lamely, apologetically.

Fludi supported his bandaged hand. "Oh, Little Mother," he scolded. "And you were going to take care of me?"

Lil chuckled from the doorway, her flashlight on both of them. "Go back to sleep," she told them.

Two days later Fludi's relatives arrived. At first Viv could not follow their conversation. Then it dawned on her. She turned to Lil and exclaimed, "Fludi's family plans to make the father of Sol pay a high price for the accident."

"A high price?" Lil questioned.

"Yes—a horse in exchange for a boy's thumb."

Viv confronted Fludi and Walan. "Is it true that you are going to make the father of Sol pay for Fludi's thumb?" She frowned her disapproval. "The accident wasn't deliberate," she added emphatically.

"It is our custom, Little Mother." Walan met her gaze steadily.

"We can't do that," Viv argued, her glasses slipping down

the bridge of her nose. "We've just been memorizing the Lord's prayer on forgiveness. We can't make them pay for an accident."

But custom was custom, until they prayed. Then Fludi turned to Walan. "Uncle, what should I do?"

"We will talk with your family," Walan answered. "I will go with you."

Armed with the Lord's prayer and with Walan as his spokesman, Fludi faced his relatives. After Walan had talked to them Fludi asked, "When I sin against my heavenly Father, how will I be able to go to him and ask him to forgive me if I don't forgive this boy?"

The theme of forgiveness won out.

It was evident to both Viv and Lil that God was working among the Tboli—not in large numbers but by ones and twos and threes—laying the groundwork for the coming of the Tboli New Testament. With no established churches, the house at Sinolon was still a base of operation for making God's plan of salvation known to the people.

Around Sinolon, trouble was gathering. The problem of land kept rearing its ugly head. Rebels from the north were in the area, looting and burning. Then Bus Dawson, the newly appointed SIL director in the Philippines, gave the order for Selanting and Vivian to "jump into the translation of the gospel of Luke with both feet."

The land problem was temporarily forgotten.

12

THE MOUNTAIN
OF HOMESICKNESS

For weeks Viv and Selanting raced against a deadline to finish the initial translation of Luke. Viv was in the middle of one day's project when she called out, "Say, Lil, how about coffee break?"

She left her desk and ambled out to the kitchen as Lil poured two cups of coffee from the metal coffeepot. As Viv picked up a cup and took a quick sip, she noticed an old woman sitting on the back steps of their house, staring out at the rain, crying.

"Why are you crying, grandmother?" Viv asked, leaving her coffee and sitting down beside the woman.

"An old man died last night," she answered. "He hasn't yet reached the other side. And now it's raining." The woman lifted her wrinkled, troubled face to Viv. "Very slippery the bridge when it rains. And his walking is feeble because of his oldness." She wiped her tears with the corner of her skirt and brushed her hand against her nose. "Do you think he will have enough food and water there?" she asked. "He can never return to his fields here."

"Oh, grandmother," Viv answered. "If he had only known Jesus. If we only had more of God's Word. . . ."

Viv's words seemingly fell on deaf ears. The old woman frowned, perplexed, her face still troubled. She stood slowly, her back bent even when she was standing. With one gnarled hand she broke off a large banana leaf near the house and lifted the makeshift umbrella above her head. "I'm leaving now," she said as she made her way down the steps to the muddy trail.

Viv watched her go. "Oh, God," she cried silently. "Why does it take so long to give them God's Word? Why are we so slow when people are dying?"

The translation team had been going full steam ahead and was still behind schedule. Now they were down to counting verses, not chapters. They were almost through the book of Luke.

More than once when stymied by the language, Viv had asked, "How can we ever say it in Tboli?"

Time indicators had to be straightened out to give the right meaning. To the Tboli, *next year* always meant the "year behind"; *last year* meant "the year ahead"; *before* meant "from below." In a language that had no need for words like "preach" and "angel," words had to be coined. For *preach*, they chose the phrase "to make known"; for *angel*, "God's messenger."

"Was Andrew the older or younger brother of Simon Peter?" Ting had asked. In Tboli, where family position made a difference, it had to be decided. Culture solved the problem when Ting said, "the one mentioned first is always the older brother."

Some time later, during one of their visits to the Nasuli center for consultant help on the book of Luke, Selanting was asked to speak at the Sunday morning worship service. Selanting appeared more relaxed than Vivian as he told his story of coming to know Jesus. "I was in grade three when I first started to live with Little Mother and Big Mother. And I knew they always prayed to God. And they taught us a prayer, the kind we memorized, but we just said it, not thinking what it meant. It was not until I was second year in high school that I really understood it."

From his shiny black hair to his sturdy bare feet, Ting held himself straight, adding stature to his sixty inches. "It was at my own mother's death, the Spirit of God spoke to me." He hesitated for just a moment and then went on. "At her funeral I taught the people from the Bible verses we had. And I told them how necessary it was to be ready to meet our God, to be ready to die. That was the first time I ever taught the Word of God."

As Viv groped for words in English to interpret his story, a half-amused smile played on Selanting's lips. "You paused too long," he told her. They both laughed out loud and started over.

Ting was shyly handsome, his teeth straight and white when he smiled. His bright pink shirt was open at the neck, his khaki pants creased in the middle. From time to time as he talked, he rested one brown hand on the table beside him. When he finished speaking that Sunday morning, he said, "There would be no Tboli children continuing their studying if it were not for our mothers here." He cast a quick identifying glance at Viv. "If it were not for them, we would not know this Jesus."

Two missionary teachers, friends of Viv, sat in the audience, listening. But Viv didn't know they were seeking meaning to their ministry in the bamboo schoolhouse at Nasuli. The teachers, both Americans, needed to stake a new claim, to have a link with a translation team and to personally care about a people in need of the vernacular Scriptures. That morning, unknown to Viv and Selanting, the Tboli team gained two new partners, Jinnie Lou, the teacher who loved to pray and sing, and Till—Jinnie's quick-tempered, red-headed roommate.

When they talked to Viv after the worship service, they asked about the Tboli, the work. "Why don't you come see for yourselves?" Viv invited. "You need to get out in one of the barrios and meet the people."

Weeks later the very goal of entry into Sinolon saw partial fulfillment as Viv prepared to return to the barrio with boxes filled with the gospel of Luke. The two schoolteachers from Nasuli, Jinnie Lou and Till, and one of the Dawson children, Gail, were going with her.

"It may not be fun but it will be an experience," Viv assured them as they boarded the Davao Express bus for Sinolon. It was both. After they piled their luggage on board and found seats inside, the bus driver put his foot on the accelerator and shot out into the darkness, rattling down the gravel highway in the pouring rain. The evening wind and torrents of rain blew in the loose-fitting windows. Jinnie tried in vain to close the window more securely.

"Comfortable?" Viv asked in jest as they huddled together on one wooden seat.

Till, the shorter teacher, lifted her eyebrows skeptically. "With the back of this bench digging in my shoulders?"

Viv chuckled. Jinnie was silent, her long legs cramped as her kneecaps braced against the crowded seat in front of her. Gail, her long, blond hair touching her shoulders, was as quiet as ever. She looked up at Jinnie and smiled shyly.

At midnight the driver tried gunning through the mudholes at a road construction site. Outside, to the right of the bus there was a deep, slushy mudbank. With one final shifting of gears, the bus tilted and jammed into a stalled truck. The driver studied the situation briefly, then turned to his passengers. "We'll wait for the bulldozer," he announced amiably. With that he promptly settled down to sleep, his snoring loud and distinct.

"We might as well try to get some rest ourselves," Viv suggested. "Dawn and the bulldozer will appear together."

At daybreak Viv and her trio of guests kicked off their shoes and were about to step from the tilted bus in search of an outhouse or a hedge when they spotted a bulldozer grinding steadily toward them.

Once the bus was pulled from the mud, they were off again, roaring down the rutted highway as if they really had a schedule to keep. An hour beyond their night's lodging they stopped again, abruptly, as the bus rounded a mountain curve into a landslide.

It was late when they finally reached the M'Lang Crossing. "We'll have to change buses here," Viv told her sleepy companions.

Soon they were jogging along in an even more bumpy vehicle. A few more unscheduled stops and a lot of dusty miles and mudholes later, they reached Sinolon. Jinnie glanced at her watch. "Wow—forty-two hours to go 125 miles."

"But arrival in Sinolon means the arrival of the gospel of Luke in Tboli," Viv responded optimistically.

Once inside the house, the younger boys gathered around Viv, eager to open the cartons of books. On each of the trial-edition copies of Luke was written: "The Good News of Jesus Christ as written by Luke."

"Good news for the Tboli in the language they know and love," Viv told the teachers. She smiled at Selanting, who was holding a copy of the new book. "Selanting and I spent months preparing this good news, months searching for precise meanings, words, expressions."

Lil and the other eight boys living with them all shared in the search for words. "Sometimes we discovered the exact word during family devotions," Lil told their guests. "Now and then we heard it at a Sunday morning service where the boys were teaching. More often it came from just living and working together."

Day after day during the teachers' visit, the translators divided themselves between two cultures. On market day Jinnie Lou busied herself teaching the younger boys the pop, pop, popping popcorn song. But Till stood by the window, watching the people wend their way up the trail to the house—a continual line of visitors, many of them carrying their sick with them.

"We have some beautiful new books at our house and some company, too," Viv called to the people as they came up the steps. But the books drew the greater attention.

As the teachers watched, Viv and Lil squatted on the floor of the porch, conversing freely in Tboli, passing out medicine, sympathizing with those with running sores, malaria, worms, bolo cuts, and anemia. They could only treat the symptoms, barely scratching the surface of human physical need.

That afternoon the Nasuli guests sat around the kitchen table with the translators and their family of boys, poring over the words of Luke. "For months we've been going through Luke, studying it verse by verse, story by story," Lil explained. "This is when it really pays off."

Gadu sat next to Jinnie Lou, half-humming, his legs swinging freely under the table. The two fifth-graders were next — Fludi as bright as a button and Alun, who had come often for lunch and stayed on as part of the family.

Across from Viv sat Kasi, their fourth-grader with the sensitive face; whenever he attempted an answer he stuttered in his excitement. Then came Bedung, who was in the last year at the barrio school. He had already told the teachers, "I speak the words of a Datu." As he sat at the table now, he seemed completely absorbed in the Scriptures. Walan, their high-school graduate, sat at the end of the table, his actions and speech thought provoking as he asked and answered questions. Mai, the extrovert, the go-getter, was sitting between Selanting and Yadan. Although Yadan was impulsive and hard-working, he was slow, hesitant at the table, shadowed by Mai's quick and ready responses. All through the study Selanting smiled, shyly elated at the book of Luke he was holding, the book he had helped to translate. Not until the end of the study did Lil or

Viv offer any suggestions or interpretations; the boys had been too busy discovering the stories of Luke for themselves.

There were others for mealtime that weekend, crowding around a table piled high with rice and corn, vegetables and bamboo shoots, and small, dry, salted fish with the eyes still in them. Juan and Rosito, two of the young high-schoolers from King's Institute, were there. And so was gentle, timid Manib, who was just as full of music as Yadan. Nga Sol came, too, with his tousled hair and bowed legs, full of singing and riddles. The table never seemed any bigger, but there was always room for one more.

Sunday morning, the boys were up the minute the sun slipped over the mountaintop, off to teaching points with the portions of Luke they had just been studying. At seven Lil urged their guests to hurry. They would be crossing the river and hiking out to a neighboring barrio with Yadan, to his preaching point forty minutes away.

Two hours later they sat on freshly swept bamboo flooring and watched sixty Tboli responding to the words of Luke. The people sang. They listened. They nodded.

In another of those eight teaching areas that day, a Datu stood up in another crowded room and said, "For a long time we have been gathering together in my house each week to call on God. But I'm ashamed that we have not built a house for this purpose. It is as if we don't feel it important for God to have his house among us. But I'm an old man, not strong enough any longer to cut down the trees and drag them in. It is up to you young men. What about it now? Are we going to get together and build this house?"

There was a restless stir and shuffle before anyone answered him. Finally there was an assent from the corner of the room. Then another. And another. When the plans had been made, Walan, who taught there that day, stood up and prayed. "You have heard, Lord, how we have been plan-

ning your house. Tomorrow the men start the work. But all
the materials we collect—the trees, the bamboo, the
grass—it is not ours. We are using what is yours to build
your house. Give us joy as we build. Make us understand
that this is not an ordinary house we are building, but a
house with a big purpose, for it is in this house that men will
learn how to be freed of their sins."

Lil, Viv, Yadan, and their guests hiked home in the heat of
the day and down the hillside to the river to bathe.
Carabaos, looking like large gray rocks, soaked in the rip-
pling stream. Women washed clothes. Families bathed.
Children swam. A short distance down the bend in the river,
Muslims took their goats to the water's edge and prepared a
blood sacrifice.

Viv and her friends sat on separate rocks in the fast-
flowing current, dressed in native tubular wraparounds,
feeling refreshed as time and the water rippled past them. "I
can't think of any place I'd rather be," Viv admitted. "It's
wonderful to watch a New Testament translation unfolding
in lives in a house bursting with boys and laughter."

Perhaps it was then, while they sat on the rocks, cooled
by the water, that the redheaded teacher said, "Someday
I'm going to write the Tboli story."

Viv laughed. The writing of a book seemed far away. But
she said, "When you do, write your book so that the struggle and the questions show through."

The day before the teachers and Gail Dawson left Sinolon, a man came running up breathlessly. "We need your
help," he told Vivian. "The wife of my older brother is
hemorrhaging after the birth of her child."

Vivian, Walan, and Till hurried over the trail to the dying
Tboli—a Tboli who had never heard that Jesus loved her. It
was a long walk, half a run, before they reached the worn
bamboo house and climbed the notched steps into an almost barren room.

They were already too late. A shriveled grandmother sat on the floor with her arms around her dead daughter. "This should have been me," she cried. "Wake up, Bo. Wake up. Your food is at your head and your baby is waiting to nurse." She put her wrinkled cheek against her daughter's face and sobbed.

The dead woman's sister crouched on the floor, rocking the baby. The infant sucked hungrily at his fist. A younger man with tear-filled eyes stood in the corner of the room, fidgeting helplessly with his bolo. Neighbors peered in the door. From time to time Viv turned to the teacher and explained what was happening. "Bo's husband is off in the fields and has not yet learned about the birth of his son or the death of his wife. A runner has been sent to tell him," Viv said softly.

"Did Bo know Jesus?" the teacher asked.

"No—no one here does."

"No hope at all?"

"None." Viv sat on the bamboo flooring, hugging her knees against her, fighting tears. "Death to the Tboli without Christ is a mountain of homesickness, a lonely journey over a rickety bridge. Once this is crossed, according to their belief, they turn only to find the bridge gone and to realize there is no return." Viv shook her head sadly.

The old mother kept crying. "My daughter has no companion to go with her on the journey." She rocked back and forth on her heels. "You were sitting with us just a little while ago, Bo. Come back. You're all alone."

When people began carrying a few of Bo's items from the house the teacher frowned. "What are they doing?"

"Preparing for the burial," Viv explained. "They will probably bury those things under the house with Bo. They'll be burning the house immediately. No one can live in the house where someone has died." Fighting her own tears, Viv scooted across the bamboo floor. Quietly she helped the mother clothe Bo in a hand-woven blouse and dark skirt. Then the old woman tenderly combed her daughter's hair, Tboli-fashion.

It was custom that guests must be fed. Cradling the baby in one arm, the dead woman's sister took an egg from the basket and gave it to Viv.

"But we did nothing," Viv protested.

"But you came," the woman said quietly.

As she shared the grief of the household, Viv was caught up in a grief of her own. "Our older boys wanted to start a teaching point in Bo's area," she said. "But I kept thinking it far too premature. I hesitated. I kept telling them we couldn't spread ourselves too far—there were too many mountains, too many Tboli."

Moments later they were outside, standing a short distance from the house, waiting, watching. A neighbor came, carrying a few hot coals balanced on his bolo. He touched these to the overhanging thatched roof. Viv turned away as the old shack—the house of the dead—ignited into flames.

The house was still burning as they started on the trail home. "Sometimes," Viv told Till as they retraced their steps to Sinolon, "we are so busy with vegetables and soap and salt and cuts and sores and diarrhea that we haven't even started the battle with Satan for the souls of all these friends of ours. The salt and soap and sores are easier."

13
SLEEPING NETS AND GOSPEL CHECKS

On a Saturday morning eight months later, everyone at the house in Sinolon sat around the table, reading about the Crucifixion, preparing for the Sunday lesson in the mountains. Gadu, who was always teasing and never a bit shy, picked up the text and reread a verse in Luke. He frowned. "Beating on the breast?" he questioned earnestly. "What is it you're trying to say here, Little Mother? Do you mean that all of these people have tuberculosis?"

It was obvious to Viv that Gadu was serious this time. She looked at the text and studied it.

"What are they pounding for?" Gadu asked again.

"The beating is a sign of their grief," Viv told him.

"But, Little Mother, my people beat for coughing spells," Gadu explained gently.

Selanting had given the right Tboli word in translation, but Gadu had caught the deeper implication. Together Viv and Selanting corrected their error and inserted the phrase, "as a sign of their grief."

Ever since the arrival of the book of Luke in Sinolon, Viv and Lil had been making changes, clarifying the meaning so that Tboli people would understand what God's Word intended. After each correction, Viv read the revision to Walan, watching for his slow and deliberate reactions. If he had a question, the translators and Walan would talk it over and search again for a word that would speak "straight" Tboli.

While Lil and Viv tidied up the kitchen that day, they discussed some of the changes that had been made. One of the younger boys looked up at them solemnly and said, "It's becoming so plain we won't even have to explain it anymore."

Viv still had twelve chapters of Luke to revise when a letter from Bus Dawson arrived. "Dr. Eugene Nida and Dr. Henry Waterman, officials for the American Bible Society, will be coming to check Tboli Luke in April," Bus wrote. "And whether you know it or not, the whole Philippine branch depends on your translation...." Then he added —half seriously, half in jest—"The proof of our Philippine ministry is hanging on Tboli Luke."

Viv looked forward to Dr. Nida's first visit to the Philippines, but deep inside she was troubled. The American Bible Society evaluation team was coming too soon. To Viv, time never seemed so short, Luke never quite so long.

"Oh, Lil. There's the house, the food, and the boys to get ready," Viv groaned.

Lil nodded. Under her supervision, the house at Sinolon would never look so good. She had jobs for everyone. The older boys swept down the roof and the walls. Vivian and Lil splurged and bought a new wire fence for the sow and her eight little piglets. Mai painted the stove and collapsible oven with aluminum paint. Three of the high-schoolers sanded and varnished the kitchen table and polished the bamboo floor with a coconut husk. The smaller boys cut the grass and hedge with their bolos and weeded the pineapple.

While Lil organized the household and handled the daily medical work, Vivian, Walan, and Selanting spent three weeks of concentrated study, readying Luke for inspection. By then it was the first Sundy in April. The people from the American Bible Society were due the next morning.

Viv was hurriedly typing up three copies of Luke when Lil appeared in the doorway. "We're short a sleeping net," Lil announced. "We just can't find one of them."

"Short a sleeping net? That's crazy," Viv exploded.

They went back to the kitchen together to quiz the boys. It came down to Mai. "Where's your sleeping net?"

"I don't have one." He avoided their gaze.

"You don't have a sleeping net?" Viv's voice was edged with impatience. Violating Tboli culture, she plunged in accusingly. "Mai, you did have a sleeping net. Every one of you has his own net."

Mai stood his ground, unbending, his face serious. "Walan and Yadan have sleeping nets. But I never had one. I had an old one of Bedung's, but I never had my own."

Viv was stunned. How could they have missed Mai? As conscious as they were of malaria and trying to teach the boys good health standards, how could they have missed? Exasperated, Viv turned and went back into the study, firmly closing the door.

At ten-thirty that night, when she thought everyone else had gone to bed, Viv was still putting in the corrections on Tboli Luke. Suddenly there was a knock on her door. Before she could speak, the door opened. There stood Mai. "You did buy a sleeping net for me, Little Mother." His voice was low and strained. "I sold mine."

Viv groaned. Not this on top of everything else! She was too tired. "Oh, Mai. . . ." She stared at him, wondering how many times they had gotten after him for giving things away or selling them; for forgetting the truth. Relatives were always asking the boys for things. If they didn't give what was asked for, they feared becoming ill, having a poor crop, or an accident. So Mai had sold his sleeping net. Viv sighed. That was Mai, she thought. Going ahead and doing things, grappling after popularity and acceptance.

"Mai," Viv said. "Just go to bed. I'm so tired of scolding you about giving your things away. And it doesn't do any good. I don't care what you do any more. Give away everything you have if you want to. Sell everything. But don't expect us to treat you like a son if you can't obey. Now go to bed, Mai. I've got so much to do I haven't time to talk about all of this."

Mai stood with his back to the wall, his head pressed against the doorpost. The Coleman lantern shadowed his glum expression. He looked at Viv without flickering an eyelash. "Don't send me out, Little Mother," he whispered. "I'm so full of sin inside; it is as if I am altogether rotten. If you can't help me, I feel as if I will die."

Viv felt herself crumple inside. She began to cry. "Mai, come in—sit down."

For Viv and Mai, nothing else mattered in all the world at that moment except getting right with God and each other. Viv, too, needed forgiveness. Long into the night they talked things out and prayed together.

After Mai had gone to bed, Viv put her head down on the desk where the manuscript lay, and sobbed. "What a miserable mother I am, God," she said. "I can hardly believe that Mai had the courage to blurt out his trouble after what I said to him. Oh, God, what good is Luke in Tboli if I fail these boys?" But the Lord's mercy in that darkened hour before dawn was sufficient for a repentant mother as well as a repentant teen-age son.

Early that Monday morning, just as Lil removed the first pan of cinnamon rolls from the collapsible oven, two jeeps bounced to a stop in front of the house. Bus Dawson's feet hit the ground before the engine was off. He turned to introduce the guests. "Dr. Eugene Nida and Dr. Henry Waterman from the States," Bus said as they tumbled out of the jeep, covered with dust.

Others followed. Dr. Gallang from the Manila branch of the American Bible Society. Don Larson and Roy Thomas from the Christian and Missionary Alliance mission. Dick Elkins, one of the SIL branch translation consultants. C&MA workers from the Bilaan area. And Len Newell's energetic, pint-sized wife, Doreen, who had come to help Lil with the pots and pans and cinnamon rolls. The folks at Sinolon had never seen the likes of such a gathering.

Right after breakfast and a bath in the river, the guests gathered around the table with Viv and Selanting, and the work began. Dr. Nida, the translation checker known the world around, sat beside Vivian. Nida had taught translation principles at the SIL summer schools and had written books on translation used the world over—books Viv had followed. Yet in five minutes he had so put her at ease that the check from start to finish was pure pleasure.

Dr. Nida instructed Viv to translate the first two chapters—the hardest chapters in Luke—from Tboli back into English, word for word. When they finished checking these, verse after verse, question after question, Dr. Nida turned to Vivian and said, ''Young lady, you've done a splendid job.''

14
PIKE'S PEAK— SHORT CUT TO TRIUMPH

For Viv, an unfinished grammar analysis was a miserably heavy load to carry year after year; it was like trekking a thousand-mile journey by foot. If Viv was ever to make the Scriptures speak clear, idiomatic Tboli, she needed consultant help. A three-month linguistic workshop at Nasuli in 1963 proved a good starter in unraveling language problems.

The Helio Courier, *The Spirit of Pontiac,* with Bob Griffin at the controls, whisked Viv, Lil, and their language helpers off from Sinolon to Nasuli. Thirty other translation teams poured into the center, making Nasuli just about the busiest place on Mindanao.

In the center of Nasuli, a row of five nipa cottages edged the dirt road. Individual homes with aluminum roofs were going up rapidly. A two-unit bamboo schoolhouse sat on the hillside. Beyond that stood the hangar, large enough for two Helio Couriers. Taut antennas rose from the radio shack, their guywires sparkling in the sun. Just beyond the row of cottages lay a bright blue natural pool shadowed by trees—the hub of activity.

Dr. Kenneth Pike, president of the Summer Institute of Linguistics, conducted the workshop. Pike, a wiry man with spectacles and an elastic, brightly expressive face, demanded a heavy schedule of classes morning, noon, and night.

Yet he never required more in his lectures or seminars than he was willing to give himself. Again and again he stimulated hope in the translators with his academic approach to Bible translation and with his Sunday morning messages on the grace of God. Each team was the Lord's channel to a whole language group. If Pike could tap the potential in each translator, it would help him tackle language data and sort it appropriately.

The language helpers facing cultural shock in this strangely academic world were as diverse as their languages: G-string-clad Bataks, numbering less than three hundred; Samal-Muslims so numerous that it would take several translation teams to reach them all; other mountain people accustomed to small barrios and harvesting in the fields all day. At Nasuli, they sat at translation tables, checking language data, verse by verse, word for word, day after day.

In these language informants and cotranslators, Pike saw more potential, and he tapped and stirred it. "These speakers of the language can produce the idiomatic expressions needed for effective translation," he told the teams.

Many informants grew homesick. Others became volleyball enthusiasts and reeling cyclists on borrowed bikes. But they were being exposed to the Scriptures in a new way. Some, on leaving this workshop, would go home personally acquainted with the Christ of Scriptures, saying as one informant did, "My thinking has changed."

At the time of the Pike workshop, only the Tboli and Bukidnon Manobo had any printed Scriptures or any boys reading and teaching God's Word. SIL Director Bus Dawson tapped Dick Elkins, the Bukidnon Manobo translator, and Viv for training as translation consultants to help other translation teams complete their work accurately, speedily.

"I don't feel much like spending my second furlough tackling a master's degree program in linguistics at Texas. Or anywhere," Viv complained.

Dick smiled. "Come on, Viv, roll with the punches. Translators and translation consultants are made, not born."

Other workshops followed Pike's. In time, the branch would develop annual conferences in linguistics and translation principles. Besides these, there would be special periods of concentrated study with guest instructors, such as Wycliffe's chief translation consultant, John Beekman, the missionary with the artificial "tick-tock" heart valve. Grammar analysis under supervision would speed Bible translation. Never again would translators be allowed to flounder alone in language study.

In the workshops, translators discovered how sentences linked to tell a story and how parallel thoughts formed paragraphs; how units of language tossed back and forth in dialogue; and how this hierarchy of building units formed the written pattern peculiar to each language.

Each workshop also had its hierarchy of leadership. Guest lecturers worked directly with branch consultants. Branch consultants worked directly with small groups of translators, helping them individually in their language problems.

At one workshop in Manila, while Viv was preparing for the advance language exam that would clear her for full-time translation, she hit a snag. She was sure that a brief talk with Elmer Wolfenden, a branch linguistic consultant, would solve it. She stopped Elmer at the breakfast table. "I have just a speck of a language problem," she told him.

They spent the whole morning and part of the afternoon analyzing that one particle, discovering short cuts on the thousand-mile grammar journey. Nothing about Bible translation was ever taken lightly.

15
THE KIAMBA
COASTAL RUN

"**Y**ou be in charge of the literacy program," Viv had suggested to Lil shortly after Lil joined the work at Sinolon.

"No way," Lil declared.

But later, during a visit to Nasuli, Elnore Lyman's enthusiasm for literacy among the Manobos sparked Lil's interest. The phonetic method was working for the Manobo. Would it work for the Tboli, too?

Adapting the Lyman approach, Lil made Tboli charts and flash cards. These formed the basis for a series of phonetically oriented primers. That summer five of the Tboli boys used the reading charts in the mountains during summer vacation. In between plowing and planting, fencing and weeding, the boys held literacy classes.

The making of primers followed. Hundreds of hours of coordinated effort went into each primer, teacher's guidebook, and supplementary reader. For a people accustomed to being illiterate, the new primers stimulated an interest in learning new things. Tboli were happily discovering the whole new world of books.

One health booklet, *The Beginnings of Our Sicknesses,* was pure idiomatic Tboli. It made a difference when the people could read the words themselves.

"Malaria comes from mosquitoes?" one reader asked.

"Diarrhea comes from contaminated water and dirty hands?" An old Tboli woman shook her head in surprise.

103

"Scabies come from not using soap when we bathe," children told their parents.

Such ideas were startling. If the translators could encourage the people to wash their hands and boil their drinking water, it would cut down on the distribution of a thousand worm pills a month.

While Lil made strides in literacy, Viv and Selanting translated the gospel of John. The book of John was harder to translate than Luke. They searched to find idiomatic Tboli expressions for "living water," "grace upon grace," "from his innermost being shall flow rivers of living water," and "bread of life." But what a good book. Viv appreciated John's words more than ever when she tried to make them meaningful to others.

Viv and Selanting had just settled at the translation table one morning when Viv looked out the window. She stared at the people coming up the bank from the river toward the back steps, a little old grandmother in the lead.

"Oh, no," Viv said to Selanting. "Grandmother will stay for hours."

Ting fell silent for a moment. He leaned back in his chair, frowning. "You know, Little Mother," he said quietly, "if you don't know how to welcome people into your house, you might as well go home no matter how beautiful this book is."

Viv's cheeks pinked immediately; retaliation caught in her throat. The grandmother didn't notice. She came gracefully into the room and sat down near Viv, all chatter. Viv, usually bubbly in return, was silent by her own guilt.

Ting came to Viv's rescue. "Grandmother," he said politely. "Do you know why we're working at this table?"

"Tell me," the old woman invited.

Ting told her the whole story of God sending Jesus to this world. He went over it again and again. As the grandmother listened, she folded and unfolded her gnarled hands, a hint of understanding lighting her wrinkled face.

They would not see her again. Days later, death came suddenly to the old grandmother before word arrived that she wanted to see Viv and Lil. But thanks to Selanting, she had heard the message of the beautiful book at least once.

It was mid-1963 before Viv wrote home to her parents, saying, "Tomorrow will see the end of typing John. Then comes the proofreading."

They were in a wonderful rut of Luke, literacy, and the gospel of John when a third partner joined the team. There would be several partners in Sinolon over the years, staying for a few weeks or months to help out before moving on to their own translation assignments. But when the team invited Doris Porter to join them, the young Californian didn't realize that practically overnight she would become the third mother to eleven boys.

Doris, a reserved young schoolteacher, was the first of a family of eight children to meet Christ personally. In time, because of her linguistic ability and goal-setting drive, the new mother, Ye' Lomi, would assume much of the responsibility of translation.

Shortly after Doris arrived, the team took a literacy survey. Walan and Selanting traveled with them on the Kiamba coastal run to Kanalo. The year before, Gadu and Fludi had spent a school vacation at Kanalo, working in the coconut groves and doing literacy instruction on the side.

The survey trip with Doris began with a four-hour, dusty bus ride to the port town of General Santos. There at the dock was a thirty-foot launch, bobbing in the water. "How do we get on board?" Doris asked.

"That way," Selanting grinned. Doris followed Ting's finger point. Short, stocky cargadores waded waist-deep in the water, back-carrying passengers and cargo to the ship.

Doris's eyes widened. "I'm too tall to ride their shoulders," she declared.

"I'm too big," Lil moaned.

Doris was still protesting when one of the carriers scooped

her on his shoulders and headed toward the launch. Just ahead of her, Viv grabbed the rope ladder and scrambled up the side of the ship.

Once safely on board with their cartons of primers, hymnbooks, and gospels of Luke, the translators looked around. The motor-propelled launch was ten feet wide. Benches lined the outer edge of the vessel. The team squeezed on the seats in the only available spaces for the slow, four-hour trip in the heat of the day.

Sun scorched their cheeks. Waves slapped against the launch as it moved along the shoreline from village to village. When they reached their own port-of-call, the launch rocked against the afternoon tide. Workmen on board swung the rope ladder over the side. Carriers from the shoreline hurried toward them. Without waiting for the carriers, Walan and Selanting leaped from the rope ladder into shallow water and slogged to the shoreline. Other Filipinos followed, stepping off the ladder between waves.

The women passengers in front of the Tboli team waited for the ripples of waves to wash from shore. They jumped and quickly ran ahead of the incoming wave. Lil was next in line, Doris behind Lil, Viv last.

"Hurry, Lil, hurry," Viv urged.

Lil paused, watching the waves roll in to shore and out again. Waiting.

Viv kept pushing. "Hurry, Lil. Hurry."

Lil jumped. Just then, the boat drifted slightly, its motor still running. A wave washing into shore caught Lil off balance, submerging her completely. A long, brown, pony-tail and a white hanky floated on top of the water.

Cries for help from the launch magnified the fear that Lil might get swept under the boat. Carriers from the shoreline splashed frantically toward the spot where she had disappeared. Before they were halfway there, Lil bobbed to the surface. Her glasses were still in place; her usual laughing eyes blinked surprise. She sputtered against the taste of salt water. By the time the carriers reached her, the wave had washed back out to sea, and Lil was standing on muddy ground.

From the rail of the launch, Viv and Doris broke into gales of laughter. In a culture where misplaced amusement was shameful, even harmful, no one else laughed. Lil, momentarily making her way to shore with carriers on each side, was still too startled by her singular method of debarkation to join in the laughter.

Kanola was a kilometer up the beach. As they made their way single file along the sandy trail, the afternoon sun slipped under a cloud. A tropical rainstorm caught them unexpectedly, full force. When they reached the village and Pastor Tau's home, they were all drenched, their clothes clinging to them.

During those weeks along the Kiamba coast, the team visited several lay pastors and small Christian and Missionary Alliance churches, sharing their newly printed materials in Tboli. The people were eager for the Scriptures, eager to learn to read them.

The team hadn't reached the halfway mark on their literacy trip when Doris came to breakfast one morning, her eyes sparkling. Smiling at Viv and Lil, she said, "Do you know, this is the first morning since I've been in the Philippines that I haven't felt homesick."

Everyone grinned.

Doris, who did not share herself easily with others, had found her niche in the Tboli ministry and was already giving herself completely to it.

16
SCOUT'S HONOR

Accompanying the progress and victories of the Tboli work were numerous and diverse obstacles. One of them was simply keeping the land for the Tboli people. Lowlanders continually threatened the mountain people and pushed them back into the hills. Now the lowlanders wanted the hills, too.

Protecting the rights of defenseless, uneducated people was a big responsibility for a handful of young men. But Mai and Fludi insisted, "Is it right for us to stand by silently when the rice and cornfields of our own people are being destroyed by cattle turned loose on the mountainsides? Or is it right for Tboli farmers to be forced to give part of their harvest to lowlanders in order to pass safely to market?"

The SILers ached with the apparent injustice around them. Over the years, several futile efforts had been made to secure land for the mountain people. Again in April 1967, the older boys contacted a lawyer in another fruitless effort to obtain a wide range of mountains just for the Tboli. At that time they did not know about PANAMIN, a governmental agency interested in the rights and needs of the minority groups in the Philippines. In time, in their little corner of the world, PANAMIN would raise its voice on behalf of the Tboli.

Other problems bothered Viv. Just before her second

furlough, she was experiencing anxious feelings over the increasing number of boys in the home. The Lord frequently had to remind her, "Enlarge the place of thy tent, and let them stretch forth the curtains of thine habitations: spare not, lengthen thy cords, and strengthen thy stakes" (Isaiah 54:2, KJV). "Let them" meant that the burden was not hers alone.

By the time Doris joined the family, Selanting was out of high school. Mai and Yadan were high school seniors. Kasi was ready to graduate from the barrio school. And four new little boys—Tunyu and Dad, Fa and Bet—were there to greet her.

Even as a little fellow, Bet—the son of a Datu—was always getting into fights, coming home battered and dirty.

Finally one day Selanting stared at Bet and declared, "Bet, I told you if you got into another fight at school, I was going to whip you."

Moments later, Bet sat on a mat, shelling corn, sniffing and sobbing, his bottom smarting. Everyone, even Fa who always took sides with him, stood around, glaring at Bet, all of them disgusted with his fighting.

That Christmas the household at Sinolon studied the account of the blind man who heard the crowds and knew that Jesus was coming. Selanting explained the story, "When blind Bartimaeus called out, Jesus knew what he wanted. But still he asked the blind man, 'What do you want me to do for you?'"

When they finished the story, Viv looked at the others. "Let's pretend that Jesus has come to our house today," she suggested. "He is going to stand in front of each one and ask, 'What do you want me to do for *you*?'"

When it was Bet's turn to respond, he was sitting cross-legged on the floor, his eyes catching Viv's. He smiled shyly and answered, "I want Jesus to keep me from fighting."

Hearing that, Viv remembered Christmases out in Blue

Grass country with the Minnesota snow and all the Grandmas and the beautiful Christmas tree and old family ornaments. It brought a lump to her throat. But even if only a few Tboli—or the boys in their own home—came to know true peace through Christ, she didn't care if she ever got to spend such a Christmas again.

Right after that Christmas in Sinolon, Viv was away, going over the work of other translation teams. When she returned, Bet looked up at her with his beautiful, big, brown eyes and confided, "I haven't been in one fight since you left."

Just before Viv and Lil flew home to the States for Viv's second furlough, Fludi summed it up for all the boys when he said, "It doesn't matter if the roof leaks," which it did, "as long as there's a mother in the house."

There would be, for Doris was staying on in Sinolon with a temporary partner. Holding the fort while the others were on furlough was a good way for Doris to learn the language and get better acquainted with the boys. More than once it would be a challenge to her authority and her leadership as well.

Gadu, the boy who had once excelled in lying, had only recently won an honor from the barrio school for being honest. It was this same Gadu, full of life, funloving, impulsive, and sixteen, who stood before Doris now, asking "Ye' Lomi, may I go to the scout jamboree in Cebu?"

Only that morning, Mr. Aguilar, the head schoolmaster, came to Doris, registration papers in hand. "Gadu is one of the boys selected to represent the barrio school at the Boy Scout Jamboree in Cebu," he said, smiling cunningly. "His expenses will be paid by the school ... except for the registration fee and a few minor things."

Doris hesitated. As Gadu's guardian, she would need to give her permission. But what could she say? The expense was not the pressing issue. Gadu loved sports. But Doris wondered silently, *How can I explain to Gadu that an honor for sports is only fleeting? That it might make the youngest boy strive vainly for the same reward?* She feared, too, the temptations that might face him in Cebu.

Mr. Aguilar cleared his throat, waiting.

"Could Gadu possibly be back in time to teach on Sunday?" Doris asked. *If he isn't,* she thought, *who will take his place?*

"I can't promise that," Mr. Aguilar responded. "It would depend on the boat . . . or there might be some meets on Sunday. . . ."

Doris stalled. But the barrio teachers and Mr. Aguilar were determined. "Gadu must represent us," the scoutmaster argued. "With his muscular build and his athletic abilities, he is a sure winner."

Mr. Aguilar arrrived on the scene a second time, Gadu and the barrio teachers at his side. "Could Gadu go if every expense is taken care of?" Mr. Aguilar asked.

The translator could not refuse permission now. The decision was Gadu's. When Mr. Aguilar had gone, Doris talked briefly with Gadu. They prayed together, seeking God's will. Then she turned quietly back to her paperwork, thinking, "Oh, God, how can any sixteen year old turn down such an opportunity? He's worked hard for it."

The next morning she heard Gadu in the boys' room, pulling things off the shelf. He packed quickly and moments later said a hurried good-bye at the doorway. Doris watched him begin the half-hour walk to the market, the weight of his luggage banging hard against his legs. From the market it would be a hot, dusty jeep ride to Marbel, the starting point for the trip to Cebu. He would spend that first night in Marbel.

But Gadu couldn't sleep. He was troubled at the prospect of going to the scout jamboree. He wanted to go, more than anything. Yet as he lay there, he questioned his own motives. Was it the competition, the love of sports, that drove him? Or did he want the prestige, the power, the glory that would accompany winning?

The next day he told Mr. Aguilar, "I want to go home." The teacher's face registered disapproval; he tried again to convince Gadu.

"My guardians don't really want me to go," Gadu explained. He couldn't tell the teacher what he was really thinking, the struggle that was going on inside.

Mr. Aguilar frowned, tapping his fingers impatiently. "But they are Americans," he argued. "The scout jamboree is important to *our* people—our school."

"I can't go," Gadu repeated softly, "because I teach God's Word every Sunday and I wouldn't be back in time. If I won . . . the wrong way, I couldn't teach my people."

Mr. Aguilar's shoulders sagged. "So you are going home?"

"Yes, I'm going home."

17

THE HOUSE IN THE GULLY

As far as Viv was concerned, there was no better way to return from furlough than on a Norwegian freighter, steaming along the Pacific Ocean at fifteen knots. The other passengers on board the *S.S. Sunnyville* were mostly veteran travelers. They talked about Europe and Tahiti and Africa the way Viv talked about Minnesota, Everett, and Sinolon.

What a life, sitting on the deck, taking stock of herself. She had been telling the woman in the deck chair beside her about the Tboli, about the work of Bible translation, about her eighteen-month furlough training as a translation consultant in Ixmiquilpan, Mexico. Viv paused, then smiled as the wintry sea winds whipped around her. "The first time Alice and I went to the Philippines, we were full of enthusiasm and anticipation. The second time we were more serious about the whole thing. But this time, ..." Viv shrugged her shoulders and shivered. "This time, I'm almost afraid."

"Afraid?" The lady asked, tightening the collar of her mink coat around her neck. "Afraid of what?"

Viv groped for words, wondering how to explain what she was really feeling inside. "I'm not afraid of speaking the language or doing the translation work, but about living what I translate."

The woman was silent. "I think your Tboli people are very lucky," she said finally.

Three weeks after docking in Manila, Viv flew from Nasuli to the barrio of Sinolon. While she had been away, the rest of the team had found land twenty-five minutes from their old location at a price far beneath what they expected to pay. Lem Sembong, the new house in the gully, was nestled among three trees, the only uncultivated spot in an area surrounded by cornfields. Viv peered through the window of the Helio Courier as it landed close to the new house on a brand-new airstrip which the boys had cleared with their bolos.

Lil and some of the boys met the plane, each one wearing a big grin. Fludi, who was taller now, had taken the school year off to tend to the crops at Lem Sembong. Selanting had started college. Yadan had a wife and son. Alun was off on his own. Bedung had married. Igi, Walan's nephew, was the newest boy at home; and Min, Selanting's younger half-brother, and Dusin, a nephew of Bedung, were on the "waiting list."

Bet was there, too, in his battered straw hat, watching Viv as she studied the new house in the gully. "It's beautiful, isn't it?" Bet asked.

Viv nodded. The house in the gully stood on sturdy posts with a thick, cogon-grass roof and shiny new bamboo walls and flooring. "And room enough for all of us," Bet told her.

On one side of the house, two big barrels were positioned to catch rainwater. The outhouse and the bodega each had a galvanized roof. Lil's chickens had a coup; the translators a study. And they all had a showerhouse equipped with a five-gallon water can, a basin and dipper, and just enough room to turn around in.

"It sure beats a half hour walk to the river to bathe," one partner commented. Viv agreed.

Viv quickly settled into the old routine, taking her turn at "skating" the bamboo floors with a coconut husk, washing clothes on a scrub board, buying vegetables, tending the sick, getting the boys off to school, handling the radio schedule with Nasuli, and taking her turn in the study house for uninterrupted language work and Bible translation.

Viv was outside the house one morning, scrubbing sheets on a washboard, when an old man with a spear stopped to watch her. Finally he spoke. "What ideas come out of your country, Friend," he said to Viv. "How easy it is to wash clothes your way."

Viv chuckled but answered politely. "True, Father. That's really true."

The medical work, Bible translation, and literacy work were going on as usual. "Every time I look out the window," Lil commented to Viv, "I see someone coming, carrying a baby on her back." Many of the babies were sick with pneumonia.

Viv was on the porch when one couple brought in their wrinkled, dehydrated infant. "How many nights has this one been sick?" she asked anxiously as she listened to the baby's deep, hacking cough.

"Just only three nights being hot like this," the mother responded.

Viv opened her mouth to protest, perhaps to warn, "Why don't you hurry and run here when the child first gets hot?"

Before the words could burst from Viv's lips, another Tboli spoke up. "Good for you, Friend," she said, sympathizing with the family. "That's the right thing to do, get medicine when the sickness is just beginning."

Viv was speechless as she prepared the Pen-strep for the baby. Once again she had been pushed against the wall of cultural clash.

One morning several days later, a young man who had learned to read at another barrio school spotted a bright red book lying on the porch railing. He picked it up and ran his finger under the title: *The Writings of Luke*. This book was new to him.

Without a word, he left Viv and Lil and went inside the house and sat down at the kitchen table. His companion, who couldn't read, sat down beside him. An hour later the young man was still reading out loud, his companion still listening. When they left the house, the reader turned to Viv and said, "Put my name on this book and put it away for me. When I have one peso, you'll see me here again."

On Sunday, the older boys were off to their teaching points as soon as the sun scaled the mountains. The younger boys went along with them to tell the story of *Little Pilgrim's Progress* to the children. Week after week, chapter after chapter. Selanting had translated the story on his own so that Tboli, too, could know of Christian's struggles to walk by faith.

On the way home from church, Bet was a few steps ahead of Viv on the narrow trail. In between slingshot practice, Bet talked of his boyhood before he lived with the translators. "Many times I remember being sick as a child. I wondered why I didn't die."

Barefoot, both pockets bulging with slingshot ammunition, his tattered straw hat smashed in the middle, his bolo clinking at his side, he asked, "Little Mother, do you think God has a purpose for me?"

"God has a plan for each one of us," Viv quickly assured him. "A very special plan."

Not long afterward, Bet completed his studies at the barrio school. He was to go on to high school at Marbel in a few weeks when, without a word, this youngster who had been with them for six years—who had wondered if God had a plan for him—left the house in the gully just to see the world.

Perhaps it was that night or another night while they sat around the kitchen table, studying the Scriptures, that they heard the put-put of a Honda coming up the trail. Bus Dawson, burned by sun and wind, was on his way to

Kalagan country to say good-bye. "Jane and I have been reassigned," he told the Tboli team. "It looks like I'll be directing the SIL aborigine work in Australia, at least for a while."

A few hours later Viv and the household in the gully gathered around Bus. He straddled the Honda and reached for the key. Walan, now grown and serious, smiled slowly. "Ma' Bong—Big Father," he said, "when we see each other again, it will not be here on earth but in heaven."

Bus considered Walan's words, then looked up at his Wycliffe colleagues. "Bring plenty of Tboli with you when you come," he told them.

It was a good admonition to the translators, for Viv's third term in the Philippines would be the hardest one of all.

18
FINING'S LITTLE WORLD

Selanting often climbed the trail to his family home, eager to tell his younger brothers and sisters the stories about Jesus. His sister Fining listened well. Although Fining's world was only as big as the mountain on which she lived, it didn't take a big world, only one winding mountain trail, to reach her with God's love.

Fining's lifestyle was simple. Her kitchen consisted of an open fire on the floor at one end of the room, two blackened pots, and a serving spoon made of coconut shell. Her plates were large, round leaves; a new plate for every meal. One weekend Fining and her sister Timud sat on the floor on either side of Viv, fingering rice from their bowls. As they ate, Fining leaned over and whispered, "Little Mother, is it true that all your pots and pans at Nasuli are shiny and new? Can you wash them just like you wash your plates?"

Fining's world was small, but her faith was large. She grew steadily, her faith mushrooming within the Tboli culture. When she married according to the custom of her people, she was eager to be a scriptural wife. On a Sunday long after her marriage, Fining and Viv hiked on the trail on their way to the mountains. Fining moved gracefully, her firstborn on her back, her wraparound skirt draped and knotted in the front, a bright yellow blouse tucked inside. Ankle bracelets twirled on her slender legs.

After an hour on the trail they stopped to rest. Fining turned toward Viv, her lovely, light brown face framed in the hair style of her people. Without any conversation leading up to it she said, "Little Mother, it's a very beautiful thing to experience, this following Jesus." Her clear, dark eyes were relaxed and smiling as she looked up at Viv.

During Viv's third term in the Philippines, Fining's simple, trusting faith bypassed pagan sacrifices and held steady, even at the death of her small son. On that fatal day Fining and her husband, Mladang, were planting rice, a five-minute, steep mountain climb from their home, where their three children were playing.

Three-year-old Nga To' crawled under a cogon-grass shelter to roast an ear of corn. He sat alone, blowing on the wood until it flamed. Suddenly the flame caught the over-hanging cogon.

To's older sister watched in horror as the thatched roof erupted in flames. "Fire, mother, fire," she screamed.

Fining hovered close to the ground, dropping rice seeds into the soil. She straightened at the cries of her daughter, listened intently, then ran. Her feet barely touched the ground as she raced up the mountainside. When she reached her son, To's feet showed through the burning cogon. Gently, Fining pulled him free.

"Water," the child whispered as she carried him into the house and placed him on pillows.

Fining squatted beside To', crying, praying. "This is your child, Father. You can give him back to us if you want to. You can take him to heaven if you want to. It's up to you." Fining rocked on her bare feet, praying softly. "We won't command you as to what you are to do. This is your little one. This is your little one."

Mladang, the stubborn, spitfire husband who had reject-ed Christian faith, crouched beside her. "Keep praying, Fining," he pleaded. "I don't know how. Pray that someone will care for To' when he reaches the bridge of death."

As the moments slipped away, Fining kept talking about Jesus and heaven. "Have you already seen Jesus, To'?" she asked.

"Already."

"Have you seen your new home—the beautiful country to which you are going?"

He opened his scorched eyelids. "Already."

"Never mind your burned skin, To'. You'll get a new body when you get there."

"Mmmmm."

Fining touched To's tattered, burned shirt. She smiled at her son. "These old worn out clothes of yours—Jesus will give you new ones, To'." She was leaning close to him, whispering softly in his ear.

To' tried to move his swollen lips. "Mmmmm," was all he could manage now.

"You wait for us there," the young mother said tenderly. "We'll come after. Don't be afraid, To'."

As the mother talked to the dying boy, Tboli gathered around, weeping. Mladang turned away, his groanings guttural, incoherent.

The boy did not cry. But three hours later, having whispered "Jesus," To' went to meet the Lord—not swaying unsteadily over the Tboli bridge of death but stepping safely into the arms of Jesus who, even in his earthly ministry, had always welcomed little children.

19
A MOUNTAIN RANGE AWAY

By 1966 the Tboli team and their SIL colleagues were beginning to see a translation explosion in the Philippines, the fruit of all those years of language learning, linguistic papers, and anthropological studies. As they saw changed lives among the people, it was well worth the effort, a thousand times over. Viv was especially grateful for what was taking place in Mai's life.

Mai, the go-getter, a young man loaded with potential, had followed the long trail back to peace. Now he lived on the top of a mountain range with his bride, his home looking down over all the Alah Valley.

At Mai's invitation, Viv had gone to that mountaintop to work on translation. As they sat together on Mai's porch, Viv thought back on Mai's long struggle. She couldn't help remembering that in a land of tropical storms and typhoons, the storms that frightened her most had often started with Mai. With each new storm, Viv had prayed for him. For hadn't she experienced the thing he was fighting—himself and his God? Hadn't she tried to run away from God when she was his age? But Viv had also experienced the goodness of the Lord which led to repentance. Wouldn't God lead Mai in the same way?

Viv's thoughts were mixed—quick sketches of Mai: his dishonesty, his running, his preaching, his praying. His impulsiveness, his laughter. His potential. His sleeping net.

She remembered the time in 1962 when Mai had multiplied his lies, hotly denying them all to Walan and the rest of the household at Sinolon. "Mai isn't right with the Lord," Viv had said to Lil. "So how can he sing God's songs? How can he pray? How can he teach on Easter Sunday?"

On that Good Friday, when Mai still needed to straighten out his life, they gathered around the table to study "The Miraculous Draught of Fishes."

Walan was reading. "Simon Peter fell at Jesus' feet crying, 'Depart from me, Lord, for I am a sinful man.'" And later Walan concluded, "When they brought their ships to land, they forsook all and followed Jesus."

Then the boys' questions started. "Could our ships represent our former lives?"

"What about the one who returns to his ship after he has begun to follow Christ?" asked the younger boy beside Mai.

"What is the result of hidden sin?" asked another.

"What makes one a fisher of men?" The questions kept coming.

Mai sat silent, his facial lines twisted in misery. As she watched his face, Viv felt a thousand mountains away from Mai. "Oh, God, how can I reach him?" she prayed silently.

The day before Easter, Mai stopped in Viv's study just before leaving the house with Fludi. "Is there something you would like to say before you go?" Viv asked.

For a moment Mai stood rigid, sullen. "There is," he said finally, his defensive attitude melting. "I've lied again, Little Mother," he admitted. "What can I do?"

"Make things right. Ask for forgiveness," she told him. And then, because Walan was the older and therefore representative of them all in the culture, she added, "I would ask forgiveness of Walan."

"But what if he won't forgive me?"

"You won't know until you ask." She smiled. "I'll go with you."

A few moments later in a room full of boys, Mai turned to Walan. Using the term of respect for an older person, he said, "Friend, Walan, will you forgive me?"

"You are already forgiven," Walan replied.

Viv's pulse raced. She was joyful. Could there be any doubt, she thought, that a victorious Easter would follow Good Friday?

There were other memories of Mai. She reflected that school had always been easy for him. In his last year of high school in Marbel, he was student body president—the first mountain boy to receive such an honor. As for Bible teaching on Sunday, he had more natural ability than the others. Recognizing his potential, barrio officials, teachers, and the mayor were all after him to become a lawyer—*the* profession of the Philippines. "Then you can help your own people," they told him.

That seed took root. He dreamed of being more than a barefoot mountain boy with nothing but a little kaingan on the hillside. More and more his ambitions had been for personal gain, personal glory. High school graduation and the start of college had been the beginning of four restless, empty years for Mai—walking independently of God.

Every time Mai made one little uncertain step back in the right direction, his younger brother Fludi was there to encourage him, help him, believe in him. But Fludi felt it keenly when Mai left to marry a child-bride as graceful as a deer.

For a while after leaving the house at Sinolon, Mai walked steadily, obediently. But by 1966 Mai was appointed barrio captain for a whole mountain area. Personal debts mounted. He was caught in the web of recognition and power. Finally, God used the serious illness of a friend's child to touch Mai's heart again.

Mai had entered the home of a friend. There was an uncanny stillness. He stared at the bundles of mats and blankets, the baskets and pots gathered by the door. "What's going on here?" he asked.

"Our baby is dying," his friend answered. "We don't want to destroy everything with the house when the baby dies."

As Mai grew accustomed to the darkness, his eyes rested on the small child lying on a mat, his mother kneeling beside him. Mai approached them. Everything that was to be buried with their baby—the grandfather's sword, small knives, a coin—was on the mat beside the dying child.

Mai crouched beside the mother, remorse gripping him. *If only my following Jesus had been straight,* he thought, *I would dare pray to God for this child. I would comfort this mother.*

The father's voice behind him interrupted Mai's thoughts. "Mai, pray for our child."

For a moment there wasn't a sound in the room. Mai looked away. Surely others had already prayed, he thought; medicine has failed. Finally Mai bowed his head and started to pray, "If the parents of this child, if all three of us can learn something from the healing of this child, then heal him for our sakes, for Jesus' sake." Then Mai stood up quickly and rushed from the house, panic-stricken that God might reject his prayer—not knowing that God was already answering.

Two weeks later Mai saw his friend again. "Your child?" he asked hesitantly.

"He's well." The father's words were the glimmering of mustard-seed faith that Mai needed to come back to his God again.

Now, as Viv sat with Mai, there was no doubt about it. Mai was being changed. Since his graduation from high school, it was the first time that he really wanted to help with the translation.

Mai had never been one who could sit for long stretches at a time and work. Up here, he could plow every morning and afternoon between translation sessions. As Viv watched, Mai's little wife moved gracefully about the porch. She stopped briefly to stare at Tboli words on paper. Then she scurried off, leaving Viv and Mai to work alone.

Viv smiled seriously at Mai. What a responsibility they shared—saying in Tboli what Luke said when he first wrote his book, searching for the words that Paul would have used if Timothy had been a Tboli. To Viv, the books of Timothy in Tboli were so applicable to life there—young fellows teaching; a church just getting started; people having to reevaluate old beliefs. She knew that translation was absolutely impossible without the direct guidance of the Holy Spirit.

The storyteller in Mai came out as they translated. He gestured as he read, as though he were teaching, his profile intense, his dark eyes flashing. "Which way sounds better now? Which word should we choose, Little Mother?" he would ask again and again.

That day as they sat on the porch, Mai read some of Timothy out loud. Then he looked at Viv and smiled. "Little Mother, it reads beautifully. Now we've got God's Word in real Tboli."

But for Viv, joy over Mai's victory would be shortlived, for Satan wasn't about to give up his territory or his youthful follower without a fight.

20
ALI'S LITTLE RED BOOK

Literacy took its toll on translation. But Viv and the rest of the team knew the most idiomatic of Tboli Scriptures would be dust-covered without readers. As the three-month literacy campaigns increased, so did the techniques of teaching Tboli to read. Literacy and teaching God's Word were clearly interlaced. Both were essential to a strong Tboli church.

During one dry season Vivian and a partner started out from Sinolon for a literacy campaign in the mountains. In their packs they carried mosquito nets, blankets, paper and pencils, and brand-new primers. The translators walked through woods, waded through rivers, and hiked over fields. The trees blocked out the sun as they made their way over the rutted trails and up one final, steep mountain slope to the village of Datal Teblow, on the grassy plain.

In spite of the long hike, they were up early the next morning. Classes at the "house for learning to read" started at six. "We want 'learning over' before the day's work in the fields begins," one of the five adult students announced.

"Then," Ye' Inggu added, "we can take our letters and words with us and we can think about them while we are working in the fields."

Classes began with the reading of Scriptures, singing, and prayer. Prayers were simple and sincere. No borrowed phrases. No unnecessary pleas. It was just a straightforward talking to a Father who cared about the Tboli, telling him about their sick babies, lost combs, land problems, and harvest time.

Small groups made it easy for the timid Tboli to ask questions. One lady, struggling with the words, sounds, and syllables, lifted her wrinkled face to Viv and whispered, "Even if you can't teach me everything, Little Mother, can you teach me just enough so I can read the hymnbook?"

The afternoon class was larger. Eleven youngsters sat in their worn clothes, their big, brown eyes shining with delight. For the first time in their lives they held new pencils, tablets, or books which they had purchased with vegetables. Vegetables also bought soap, combs, and worm medicine, all part of the curriculum.

Chalk dust smudged the nose and chin of the student nearest Viv. As he listened to her dictation drill, he clutched an eraser made from pillows of kapok in his left hand. With the other, he gripped a broken piece of chalk and slowly printed the letters on the makeshift chalkboard. Now and then Viv caught him stealing a glance, as new learners were prone to do, to see if his own letters matched the ones of the student beside him. Finally there was a look of joy on the youngster's face. A handful of letters had formed a word that spoke clearly to him in Tboli. "I know that word now, Little Mother. I know that," he exclaimed.

It was a small beginning, a handful of children and a few adults out of the 40,000 Tboli. Insignificant? Viv wondered. To others, perhaps, but not when she saw people like the Father of Udus, the oldest Tboli to read the book of Paul's letters to Timothy and Titus. Afterward he told the translators, "I couldn't keep the tears from dropping when I read that book." After reading Luke and Acts, combined now, he wrinkled his brow and said, "This is a book I must read many times. There is so much for me to learn in it."

The translators learned, too. They were conducting another literacy campaign in Bedung's mountain home when they met twenty-year-old Ali. Ali struggled haltingly, earnestly through each word and each sentence with no evidence of understanding. The translators had just about given up on him. But they felt a sense of disappointment when the campaign was over. They had no certificate of achievement for Ali, even though he had never missed a class and had tried so hard. All they had to give him was his little red book of Luke and Acts.

Long after the girls went down the mountain, Ali stuck with learning. The little red book went everywhere with him. When he was out plowing and his carabao had to rest, Ali sat down in the palm shade and pulled out his book.

Months later, Ali stopped at the house at Sinolon on his way to market.

"How are you doing in your reading?" Doris asked dubiously.

"I'm doing fine. I've been reading in Luke," he replied enthusiastically.

"Reading Luke?" she countered. Her eyebrows raised quizzically. "Why don't you come in and read to us?"

Ali followed her to the kitchen table, where the other translators were eating lunch. He sat down shyly beside Doris and drew out his book of Luke and Acts, dirt-edged now from where he had leafed through its pages. He held the book in his work-worn hands and began to read. The words flowed accurately, without a pause. His face registered understanding.

The missionaries listened and swallowed their surprise as they heard the words of Luke from Ali's lips. Their own mustard-seed faith was shouting at them, reminding them that God was not limited to three-month literacy campaigns. God himself was preparing a people for reading his Word in their own language.

Through the boys like Bedung in their home, through the plodders like Ali, through the Tboli themselves—men who only a year or two before had been illiterate—literacy would spread from Tboli to Tboli, from mountain to mountain.

21
BAREFOOT IN
THE PALACE

Even as the team continued the literacy outreach and translation of the New Testament, the land problem was never far away. In 1968 the lowlanders' encroachment on Tboli land seemed insurmountable. That year Doris Porter footed the bill for an encounter with royalty when she took two Tboli girls to Manila to dance in the presidential palace.

The event began March 7, when Rafael Salas, the executive secretary of the Philippines, visited Nasuli. Doris was finishing the second month of a linguistic workshop when Secretary Salas arrived. The SIL director invited Doris's colorfully dressed language helpers to present leis to the secretary and his party. What could be nicer than to have two representatives from the minorities host a typically Filipino custom?

Later, during a Nasuli luncheon, Blina and Madiya danced for the secretary, jewelry flashing and twirling on their arms and legs. Secretary Salas was charmed by their shyness and talked to them at great length, with Doris interpreting. "I'm sure," he declared, "that the president would like to meet these girls."

He invited Blina, the younger sister of Gadu and Tunyu, and Madiya, Mai's wife, to visit Ferdinand Marcos. Doris hardly dared believe that she and the girls would actually gain an audience with the president of the Philippines!

March 13 dawned like any other morning. Blina and

135

Madiya had already returned to their mountain homes near Sinolon. Doris was seated at her desk, winding up her linguistic paper. At 8:15 there was a slight knock at her door. She looked up to find SIL Associate Director Tom Lyman standing in the doorway, grinning from ear to ear.

"Could you be ready in a half hour to fly down to Sinolon and get Blina and Madiya?" Tom asked.

"Why?" asked the busy translator.

Tom grinned again. "They have an audience with the president."

Doris's thoughts raced ahead. It was a two-hour round trip by Helio Courier to Sinolon and back. It would take another three-hour hike up the mountains to get the girls, and at least two hours getting back down to the plane.

"I guess I could do with a change in pace," she said. She quickly shuffled her linguistic papers into a neat stack on the desk, pushed back her chair, and followed Tim.

The JAARS pilot canceled all other flights to take this priority flying for the day. As the Helio Courier swooped low over the mountains for a mail drop, Doris's rock-weighted message fell to the ground with its urgent request: "Come down the mountains. We are going to take you to Manila."

"If the girls are home, they can read the note and come down the mountain to the airstrip. If they're not home...." Doris shrugged her shoulders as she talked with the pilot. "They're the only ones in this area who can read."

They would learn later that the note dropped right in Blina's yard. Walan, who was providentially visiting in the village that day, picked it up, opened it, and read the first paragraph. Then he yelled, "Blina. Madiya. Get your things ready...."

Everyone was so excited that Walan forgot to read the rest of the message: "Put a big X on the ground if everything is understood."

The pilot circled and circled, waiting for the sign. Finally he said, "We'd better go back to the airstrip and land."

When they reached the house at Sinolon, only Kasi and Bedung were home. Doris quickly told them what had happened. Kasi the stutterer was off at once, racing for the mountains to be sure that Blina and Madiya were on their way.

In an hour Kasi was back with two perspiring girls. Their feet were dirty from the fields where they had been weeding. Strands of jet-black hair hung loosely. Kasi carried their little bundles of clothes as they came up the front steps with him.

"Kasi met us at the foot of the mountains," Blina said breathlessly.

A few days later, Doris and the two Tboli girls arrived at the presidential palace in Manila for their half-hour audience with the president of the country. Guards were everywhere. Black limousines pulled in and out of the driveway.

Blina's eyes widened to massive brown circles as the huge doors of Malacanang Palace swung open. She looked at Doris for reassurance before they made their way expectantly up the wide, carpeted stairway. Neither Blina nor Madiya looked up or down, to the right or to the left. Dressed in their native costumes with wide brass belts tight around their waists, they moved slowly, softly, like queens who had lived in such splendor all their lives. As Doris ascended behind them, Blina reached out for Madiya's hand. They clutched each other's hands the rest of the way, their bare feet stepping gracefully up the carpeted stairs, their decorative ankle bracelets tinkling as they moved.

Shortly after 9:30 they were shown into the president's office where, Blina and Madiya danced barefoot on the open terrace. President Marcos smiled his pleasure. When they finished dancing, he asked them about themselves and their people. Then, looking at Doris as well as the girls, he asked, "What is being done for the Tboli?"

After answering his questions, Blina and Madiya presented their president with handwoven blankets. "For you, Mr.

President," they said in English as Doris had taught them. And then, reaching their hands up gracefully, they quickly removed necklaces from around their necks and their horsetail earrings and handed these to the President. "For Mrs. Marcos," they told him.

Back down the stairs they went, the excitement somehow diminished. But God didn't take this trio to Manila only for the excitement and publicity involved in an audience with President Marcos. God remembered their prayers for help in solving the land problems in Tboli country. Through previous contacts with government officials, SIL had met Manuel Elizalde, aide to the president on the cultural minorities. While Doris was still in Manila, the SIL director suggested that perhaps this was the time to talk to Mr. Elizalde about the land problems.

As a result of their meeting, Elizalde assigned two of his topnotch lawyers from PANAMIN to investigate the situation. For two years the young men in the house at Sinolon had tried to work through a local lawyer, with no results. Now, in a matter of minutes, help from the top was on its way.

True to their word, shortly after Doris and the girls returned to Sinolon, the PANAMIN lawyers arrived. They spent one night at Sinolon, questioning the older boys and answering questions. They made no fancy promises but presented the difficulties that would have to be faced in obtaining land.

As a result of the lawyer's report, the Bureau of Forestry was asked to survey the mountain area and set aside a Tboli reservation. According to records in the Bureau of Forestry, the proposed area for survey had never been legally titled. Yet large areas where the Tboli had always lived had been "claimed" by prominent, influential cattle ranchers. These cattle ranchers were ready to go to drastic ends to keep the survey from going through. There were threats and bribes from every side and unexpected opposition from local government offices.

In early September, six months after the initial contact with PANAMIN, Aladin Repancol, a twenty-two-year-old Ilocano surveyor, arrived from Manila. He was a university graduate, youthful but businesslike. Aladin was there to secure the land for the Tboli. Threats from the cattle ranchers mounted.

The translators, who watched from the sidelines, sought the Lord's protection for the surveyors. From Psalms 124 and 140, one promise in particular came alive and danced across the written page: *The Lord will maintain the rights of the poor.*

On 11 September, Aladin and his survey party of eight Tboli, including Mai, Fludi, and Kasi, left the house at Sinolon to determine the boundary lines for a reservation. The next day they were arrested! Two days later they were released in response to a sixty-word telegram from the president of PANAMIN and the Bureau of Forestry, authorizing the survey.

The survey went on—through fourteen large cattle ranches. Time after time Aladin sat with the ranch "owners," listening to their side of the story. Then he countered, "Where do the hundreds of Tboli families go from here if the cattle take over the mountainsides? What other means of livelihood do they know?"

The ranchers sat with guns on each hip. Aladin, hollow-cheeked and small in stature, sat unarmed, talking calmly. "If you harm us, we will be replaced," he told the ranchers. "This survey is being done by the order of President Marcos."

God's plan for the survey trip included more than boundary lines. His Spirit reached into the homes along the way, to the people in those homes who had not yet heard the good news of Jesus Christ.

Each night after tramping up and down the mountains all day, Fludi and Mai gathered the people together. Everyone came. Mai taught the people hymns and Bible verses. He read God's Word and explained it and taught the people how to pray. Fludi, his faith unquenchable, encouraged them with the news that PANAMIN was attempting to get land for all of them. More and more, God seemed to be thrusting Fludi into the foreground to bear the standard for his people.

Aladin, who came to Sinolon a skeptical young man, found himself being challenged and stirred by Fludi's faith. When he saw that Fludi not only understood God's Word but was earnest in obeying it, Aladin began asking questions. One evening toward the end of the survey, the two of them were sitting by an open fire, roasting corn. As they crouched beside the flames, they took turns reading from 2 Corinthians. When Aladin read aloud of a Christian becoming "a brand new person inside," he broke into a smile. He looked at Fludi and said, "This explains what has been happening to me. I'm experiencing this change inside."

Shortly before he left the Alah Valley to return to Manila, Aladin confessed to those at the household, "It is for sure that I have been reborn here in Mindanao."

As the household in Sinolon waited for Aladin's reports to be properly processed in Manila and for the president's seal to officially proclaim the survey area a reservation, the threats from the cattle ranchers continued. Although other Tboli had gone on the survey trip, Satan's darts of opposition seemed aimed directly at Mai and Fludi.

22
BLUEPRINTS TO CHANGE

Marge Moran, the nurse from North Dakota who would be evacuated from Sinolon with Vivian in 1974, spent her first term in the Philippines as a bookkeeper. She was the last mother to join the Tboli team. The arrivals of Marge and Aladin, the PANAMIN surveyor, were almost simultaneous.

In the beginning there had been nothing earth-shattering about Marge's thoughts toward the mission field. She had graduated from Good Samaritan Hospital in Rugby, North Dakota. Later, while working as a bookkeeper for the Billy Graham Association in Minnesota, a friend asked, "Have you ever considered joining the Wycliffe Bible Translators?"

Marge hadn't. She hardly knew Wycliffe existed.

When she arrived in Sinolon, Selanting's curly haired half-brother, Min, and Dusin, the new first-grader, were already part of the family. Selanting was practice-teaching. And the rest of the Tboli team had just engineered a new outhouse, guaranteed to be odorproof and flyproof, or their money back.

The new partner was a little on the roundish side, with a full face, short, dark hair, and a happy chuckle all her own. She would be a steadying buffer in the days ahead, when the hopes for PANAMIN took an unexpected turn.

Months after Aladin's survey, Secretary Manuel Elizalde, the director of PANAMIN, visited Sinolon. Elizalde was one of the youngest members in the presidential cabinet. He had been educated in both his own country and at America's Harvard University. He had poured thousands of pesos of his own inheritance into the work of PANAMIN.

"We hope you'll like the Tboli," one of the translators said offhandedly.

Elizalde's dark eyes smiled in response. "If I do, then I'll push the reservation project through to completion—is that it?"

The translator laughed but offered no reply.

They took Elizalde to see a newly constructed bamboo schoolhouse nestled on the proposed reservation site. The short, masterly Filipino stared at the flimsy construction with its grass roof and dirt floor. He rubbed his thumb against a stubble of beard, his dark eyes flashing as he peered through the slits in the bamboo wall.

The same translator's defense of the Tboli surfaced. Somewhere in their conversation, she managed, "That building gives countless barefoot mountain children a chance to learn."

Elizalde threw her a quick, twisted grin, then surveyed the surrounding land, apparently sizing up its possibilities, its political implications.

Two weeks later, at Elizalde's order, PANAMIN teams began moving into the area—surveyors, carpenters, engineers, and a medical team equipped to do minor surgery. The carpenters came to rebuild the school with sturdier walls and a cement floor. Blueprints for the new village of Kemotu called for a fully equipped clinic, a cooperative where Tboli could buy and sell for fair prices, and plans for a road so Tboli produce could be marketed. Legal help would be available for land problems. But there wasn't much hope that the original reservation would ever go through; there were too many ranchers opposing it.

Elizalde surveyed more than the land. He singled out

Selanting, Fludi, Mai, Alun, and Yadan to get the project underway. For these young men, it was no small thing to have the son of one of the wealthiest men in the Philippines inviting them to share in the success of Kemotu. They jumped in with both feet, working from dawn to dark seven days a week. It wasn't long before Selanting assumed the teaching responsibilities in the village. Then Fa left Sinolon for the glitter of all that PANAMIN offered its followers. Even Bet, the boy with the slingshot, soon found his way down the mountainside to the new barrio.

PANAMIN demanded all their time. From the very start of the project at Kemotu, the older, married boys stopped teaching on Sundays. As the village grew, positions of leadership and authority continued to open, and many of the boys were lost completely to Bible translation.

Momentarily it seemed to Viv as though the walls of faith—the pillars of the Tboli church—were crumbling all around her. "What crushed us most," Viv confessed in a letter home, "was how easily some of the boys gave up teaching God's Word each Sunday, a responsibility they have carried steadily for years."

As far as Viv was concerned, the year before Kemotu had been the best year in translation—nine New Testament books ready to be printed and tested. Had Satan seen enough faith in the mountain ranges to throw all his forces into the battle? Had he heard God's Word speaking too clearly in Tboli? His tactics caught Viv and the household at Sinolon off guard. They momentarily forgot that even in Nehemiah's day the building of the wall and the battle with the enemy went on simultaneously until the work was completed. So it would be in Tboli land.

Early in the PANAMIN project, Fludi, the Tboli standard-bearer, had been elected barrio captain in charge of the problems brought to him. Problems came by the hundreds from far and wide. One day in December, Fludi awakened to gnawing abdominal pains. He stood, his legs unsteady. A sudden wave of nausea doubled him over and sent clammy shivers up his spine. He rushed for the porch railing and retched blood.

After vomiting blood all day, Fludi was carried to the hospital. A few days after Christmas, when he felt stronger, he visited the translation team for the first time in many months. They talked all day—praying, crying, arguing.

"It's not right," Viv told him. "You haven't taught God's Word for months."

Fludi's dark skin was still paled. He looked at Viv. "Do you think I don't care that no one is teaching God's Word at Kemotu?" he countered.

"What else can we think?"

"You can think as I do that God gave me this position of leadership at Kemotu," he answered.

As they talked, it was obvious to the team that Fludi was still determined to follow the Lord. They sensed that he needed them to stand behind him. To trust him. But they were aware, too, that he was making many little compromises—bargaining to keep the barrio help for the Tboli.

23

THE BLOWING
OF THE WIND

Life became a turmoil for the household at Sinolon. Even the small boys seemed restless, disobedient. "It isn't much fun, plowing and planting and harvesting all alone," one of them said as he stood in the open doorway.

Viv nodded and reflected, "Not when your big brothers are living in the glitter and excitement of the new barrio."

The uncertainty hit the translators, too. In a letter home, Doris unwittingly summed up the struggle when she penned a scratchy P.S. on the edge of one page: "Would you please send me some Anacin for Christmas?"

Viv's struggle was more evident. For a few days she couldn't eat or sleep or think about anything except her disappointment. She couldn't believe what was happening to Mai.

From the beginning PANAMIN had Mai. On Manuel Elizalde's first visit to Sinolon, the secretary's flashing dark eyes had sought for key men for the PANAMIN project. Mai—stocky, good-looking, clean-shaven, and eager—seemed a good choice for a contact. At last Mai was on his way to the power and acceptance he sought.

Later, when officials threatened to remove the government's help from the Tboli, Mai quickly made his choice to give up preaching. In return, he was offered a position of authority in the project. As Mai proved his abilities beyond all expectations, he became the recipient of special gifts and privileges from PANAMIN, inlcuding a Honda, a personal gift from the secretary. Future trips by air would take Mai far beyond Manila to Europe and exciting places that few bare-foot mountain boys ever see.

Viv's disappointment mushroomed. Mai had spent months at the translation desk with her in the mountains and with Doris in the valley. Had the words of Scripture burned themselves into Mai's heart and life? Viv could not be sure. She kept praying that Paul's advice to Timothy might stand out in his heart and mind as though Paul had written the words for Mai himself. "Now, *Mai*, my son . . . fight well in the Lord's battles . . . cling tightly to your faith in Christ and always keep your conscience clear, doing what you know is right. . . ."

Viv and the team struggled as if they were in the battle alone, forgetting, in the anguish of their own disappoint-ment, that getting the Bible into Tboli was God's work. Christ had assumed the full responsibility for it at Calvary. God simply offered the team a chance to participate—on his terms.

In a letter home Viv wrote, "The waves are boisterous around us. But Jesus himself is standing on the shore—not just on the Sea of Galilee but across the Alah River—waiting for that fourth hour when he is going to come walking on the waves to help us."

Over the years there had been hints of the spiritual war-fare the translators faced. But the concern for land often veiled the greater battle. The translators and the authority at Kemotu were like two opposing forces, each striving to meet the needs of the minorities. PANAMIN sought to improve the material status of the people, to blend them in with the growing nationalism. The translators, foreigners at best, sought primarily for the salvation of the Tboli in the moun-tain ranges surrounding them.

During those days of conflict, Viv's anger and prayers merged. One afternoon as she sat in her room, she half-prayed, half-protested, "Not Mai, God. He's our right-hand man when it comes to translation. None of the other boys come close to his ability. . . ."

It seemed to Viv as though her prayers bounced back from the thatched roof, mocking her. Outside, the sun was shining. There was just enough wind by Viv's open window to make the bamboo sing and whisper. The sound was off-key and frightening. Blue gray clouds drifted down like a blanket over the mountains.

As Viv sat there, she thought of the storms they had weathered over the years. But this new storm with Mai frightened her most. It was as though he had made a cold, calculated decision to walk out on God, quietly closing the book he had helped translate.

24
FLOWERS AROUND
THE OUTHOUSE

As the PANAMIN project continued to develop, one by one the younger boys turned toward the wide, well-kept road leading to the new barrio. Kemotu was backed against the foothills, lodged in a nook of abundant streams and springs an hour-and-a-half hike from Sinolon. Row upon row of houses with unfamiliar Tai-shaped roofs stretched across the village. Each home boasted a bamboo fence around it and running water from an underground pipeline. A string of electric lights, energized by a 100-kilowatt generator, ran down the main street. Close to the center stood a small clinic, a coop store, and the school where Selanting taught.

Across the river stood a forlorn bamboo church with grass high around it—a mocking monument to a way of life that had brought peace but no spontaneous prosperity. Hardly a man involved in the PANAMIN project had attended church since September. Everyone worked on Sundays. When Viv thought about the empty church, she wondered, *Should the household at Sinolon attempt to defend the Almighty? Or will he not, in his own time, his own way, defend his own honor?*

A year after PANAMIN bulldozed land for the new barrio, Lil was deep in the preparation of a teacher's manual. Marge and Doris were off to the mountains for literacy classes. Viv was becoming more involved in translation— consultant responsibilities. Selanting had a son. And the Tboli project was making headlines in Manila. According to the newspaper reports, the real issue behind the Kemotu project was the mountains, rumored to be rich in gold and uranium. The Tboli were caught in the crossfire.

Early in 1970, Elizalde asked the team to help in the clinic. "PANAMIN has the best medicine that money can buy," he told them. "But that doesn't bring in the Tboli who are sick. No matter how much money we spend, we can't buy personal concern for these people."

Although they stood on opposing grounds in their ministry, the secretary apparently recognized that the translators cared for the people. They knew the language. They sought no gold or uranium. As they talked together, he asked if the team would also start a literacy program at Kemotu. "If you ladies get a teacher-training program underway, I'll see to it that stations are set up throughout the whole area to get these people literate."

This time it was not the boys being tempted. Tboli land needed readers. The offer sounded good. But PANAMIN was political. Dared they get involved?

As they visited, one of the team mentioned Bible translation. A frown shadowed Elizalde's face. "You're wasting your time," he said frankly.

Doris countered gently, "Did you know that many of the principles you live by and use in your work are principles Jesus laid down in the New Testament?"

Surprise, then amusement showed in the secretary's expression. He paused before asking politely, "Is there a Bible that a nonreligious fellow can read and understand?"

"We'll give you one," Doris promised.

He was thoughtful for a moment. "Well, if you give me one," he said, his dark eyes hinting at a smile, "I'll try to read a thousand words a day. I ought to have time for that."

The girls would keep their promise. They could only hope that the secretary would keep his as well.

Throughout 1970, the older boys appeared at the house from time to time. When Selanting arrived unexpectedly one Sunday, Viv was the only mother at home. As they talked she reproached him for no longer teaching on Sundays. Ting exploded.

"How do you know how much I've been witnessing to the people?" he asked angrily.

Viv tried to reason, her words coming out blunt and crooked in Tboli. If she had been speaking in English, she could have made her words more courteous and respectful. When Ting left, Viv was trembling. She was frustrated by her own fury, distressed with Selanting.

Only days later Selanting and his wife arrived with gifts. A necklace for each of the mothers was the Tboli way of saying, "There are no bad feelings from our side."

Not long after, even though doctors were available at Kemotu, Ting arrived on his motorcycle. "I need medicine for my son," he told them. Later, as he held a bottle of medicine in his hands, he added softly, "Since we talked, Little Mother, several people have come to my house and asked me if I would teach them again on Sundays."

His drooping spirits lifted. But not for long. Kemotu rose to meet this new challenge. Shortly, Ting would be appointed secretary to the head man in the PANAMIN project.

Again, many months later, Selanting sent word that he wanted to quit the government project and return to translation. Another of the translators, alone that day and still smarting from the hurt of it all, sent back word, "Never mind. We're almost through."

The other team members didn't agree. There were so many things left to finish. A dictionary file of Tboli words. Some Old Testament stories. The last few books of the New Testament. The final New Testament revision and polish.

They did need Selanting's help, and what was more, Ting needed to get back into God's Word. Now it was too late. Once again they had stepped across the boundaries of culture and shamed a Tboli.

As the team sorted out what was happening, they became more aware that the distance between the boys—the young men—from their home and themselves was not a generation gap but a cultural one. As they reflected on the underlying philosophy of the East, it differed from their own. By Tboli standards, it was the translators' responsibility to share what they had with the poor. It was the Tboli right to accept help without emotional obligation. Within this culture, the one who had, gave. His reward? Prestige.

Because of this reciprocal relationship, while they lived with the translators the boys worked the cornfields and helped to meet the school expenses. According to the cultural beliefs, the obligation, if it existed at all, was therefore paid. They didn't owe a thing. When something better came along, the boys took it without visible hesitation. To them it had nothing to do with Christianity. It was custom.

Just as the Tboli ideas about honor varied from Western beliefs, so their ideas on marriage were equally conflicting. While translating Paul's advice to Timothy, "Tell young widows to marry and have children," Viv kept writing the words down. Mai kept striking them out. "What other reason to marry, Little Mother," he had questioned. "What else is there to marriage but to bear children and work the fields?"

For a few Tboli, more than one wife was a cultural status. The more wives, the greater the husband's political advantage, much like it must have been in David's time. Mai was the first of the young men from the household at Sinolon to take a second wife, and eventually a third and a fourth. Every one of his wives came from a different geographic area, thus giving Mai prestige and recognition in each barrio. It may have been lust, but it was politics, too.

The Tboli team kept in the Word, plugging away at translation. But after Gadu's younger brother Tunyu ran away, and after both Walan and Bedung got temporarily involved in the PANAMIN project, the real test came. Fludi, who had been so steady, so Christlike, fell into sin. The team had prayed night and day that Fludi wouldn't marry the teenager whose parents had used her like a piece of property, marrying her again with each dispute over the dowry. Fludi's own family scolded and fretted, pleading with him not to marry her, but to no avail.

For Viv, Fludi's fall was the hardest of all. Fludi was the boy they had hardly had to scold in the ten years he lived with them. Viv had rarely been able to count on Mai. But Fludi—Fludi had been miles ahead of all the rest, steady as the Rock of Gibraltar, with a happy faith in God. Now visitor after visitor who came for medicine repeated the story of Fludi's fall. Viv wept each time.

For days it was difficult for her to type up the newly translated Scripture portions. Her constant flow of tears blurred the copy. She churned inside; her prayers were one long crying complaint. "With all your power, God, why couldn't you have kept Fludi? Where are you, anyway? Why didn't you care enough to intervene? If all our leaders are going to fall into sin, who can stand? What's the purpose of it all?"

By the third day of weeping, Viv glared at the portions of Tboli Scriptures at her fingertips. She was ready to toss the translation out the window when Gadu came up behind her. "Fludi has his sin, Little Mother," Gadu said sternly. "But you have yours, too."

Gadu, the bouncy Peter Rabbit of the household, had his own thin line between patience and impatience, between acceptance and rejection. He had seen the glitter of PANAMIN, like flashing neon lights offering him a prosperous way of life. He'd struggled with seeing his younger brother Tunyu and friends leave for Kemotu. He stood there now, glaring at

Viv, his almond-shaped eyes reproachful as he watched her. "It's been long enough, Little Mother. It's time to get back to really working again."

Tears of self-pity washed Viv's cheeks. She stared back at the familiar triangular face, serious and hurt, disappointed in her. Then she heard Gadu's voice again pleading with her. "You're wasting time. It's time to quit thinking about Fludi's sin and start doing something about your own— you're not trusting God."

Gadu told her to get out of the house and start weeding in her flowers again, to get hold of herself. Marge was there, silenced momentarily by Gadu's outburst. But she backed him up. Their mutual scolding was the medicine Viv needed. Then God added his own.

Viv stood up and walked to the back door and down the back steps, her eyelids still swollen. Out in the yard, she looked around, then headed for the bamboo outhouse. It was the only place where she could be by herself. How often she had stayed out there longer than she needed to, sometimes just reading an old magazine, relaxing a bit. Everything was in English out there.

At the end of the path she paused and studied the flower bed bordering the outhouse. How many times she had weeded and dug around those flowers, coaxing them along, with hardly a flower or two to show for her effort. But this morning there were fifty blossoms flourishing in the sunshine. She leaned down and touched a pretty pink blossom. As she cupped the flower, it was as if God himself whispered, "Everything is all right. I'm weeding, too."

Crouched by the flowers, Viv thought of how willingly she had given herself to the Lord back at Deaconess Hospital. For a moment, she was ashamed of her years of service in the Philippines. Doing things out of real love? God had seen so little of that. Willingly accepting whatever he sent? He'd seen so little of that, too. But he had seen so much complaining, so many fears and anxieties. "Yet you knew all that on the day that you called me," she whispered. "You knew I'd fail. You knew that our team would have its differences. Its problems. But, dear God, you also knew that your Son living in me would not fail. Forgive me."

Her tears were cleansing now. For the first time in months the whole miserable burden was gone. She felt forgiven, free, and convinced that the cultural gap and the cost of forgiveness to others were partial payment on the Tboli New Testament. She felt buoyed and grateful.

25

THE ECHO
OF A SONG

From the time Viv's little portable pump organ rang out with music in the first house at Sinolon, the boys loved to sing. One of the first songs in the Tboli songbook was "Jesus Loves Me." The songbook kept growing, keeping pace with all the other work. Over the years the household at Sinolon had been through some battles, gathered some scars, experienced the Lord's power to deliver—and it showed in their singing.

Singing fit right into the culture. The boys had often shared the Gospel stories through singing, much as the Tboli had passed on their own history from generation to generation. It could be raining outside, but inside the bamboo and cogon-grass house there was always music.

Even now the picture at Sinolon wasn't completely dark. Four older boys and three younger ones were still teaching each Sunday. People up in the mountains were still attending church—listening, believing. Hundreds of Tboli had found a home in the new barrio. The roof of the house at Sinolon leaked, but, oh, what the rain had done for the papaya, avocado, pineapple, and mango! The orange tree bent low with fruit, and the flowers around the yard bloomed in every color.

In spite of the talk about land problems and Kemotu, the team was still in the business of translating and making progress, too. Viv and the team would have preferred Mai, Fludi, and Selanting for Bible translation, but God measured with a different plumbline. He was still reaching individuals. For a people who knew nothing about altar calls and sawdust trails, Tboli were nevertheless responding to God's Spirit.

After breakfast one morning, Min lingered in the kitchen with Vivian, drying dishes. "I saw Fa up in the mountains yesterday," Min told Vivian. "And Tunyu."

"Are they coming home?" Viv asked softly.

"I told them that our mothers want them to come back."

Viv smiled. It was true. Although their concern sometimes seemed sporadic, the team prayed earnestly, daily, that at least some of the boys might find their way back home.

She glanced at Min, the only curly haired boy in their lot. He and Gadu had both felt miserable, touchy at the absence of their brothers—Min's big brother Selanting and Gadu's younger brother Tunyu. Min's guard was down this morning, his boyish concern showing through. He reached for another dish, his towel too sopping to dry it.

"I told Tunyu and Fa what we say in our prayers for them . . . what we say at the table about them. . . ."

"Then they know that we want them to come home?"

"I will tell them again."

It would be hard, Viv knew, for either of the boys to come back; harder perhaps for Tunyu. Fa had asked permission to leave for PANAMIN. Tunyu hadn't.

Long after Fa and Tunyu finally found their way back home, the men in Bedung's barrio spent three days damming up a small, rocky river for a baptismal service. That Sunday, after hearing God's Word in a small, grass-roofed, no-walled church at the foot of the mountains, the people made their way to the river's edge. There, one by one, forty-two Tboli stepped into the cold waters, announcing to those around them that God was real, that Jesus did indeed live and speak Tboli. But the biggest surprise of the day for the translators was when Fa, their third-year high-schooler, stumbled forward to be baptized.

Deep, uncontrollable sobs shook Fa as he tried to tell what running away from God was like. The fun, the fleeting exhilaration of rebellion, the intermittent misery, the increasing heaviness—it all poured out. "But always right behind me I could hear Jesus following, no matter to what thing I turned, no matter which direction I ran, always he was right there behind me, always following me."

Before those who knew him so well, Fa again committed his life to God. He kept saying, "I know that God has a purpose for me right here among you. I know that for sure." Nevertheless, the old high-school gang and the lure of PANAMIN would be close behind Fa, tempting him all the way.

There was another bright spot in life at Sinolon. Boxes of clothing for the Tboli arrived frequently from a two-point Lutheran parish in Wisconsin. The boys dragged the parcels home from the makeshift post office in Surala on the cowsled—Tunyu and Fa, Min and Igi, Gadu or Walan beaming as they arrived at the house.

On one occasion, Igi grinned up at Viv as she stood in the open doorway. "Three boxes this time, Little Mother," he called.

Igi and Min carried the boxes into the house, eager as always to cut the strapping tape and open the well-packed cartons. They emptied the contents onto the kitchen table, where Marge carefully sorted the items . . . shirts, trousers, baby clothes. Everything was repaired, ironed, folded, packed neatly.

"As always they've packed these boxes with love and prayed them over to us," Viv said, holding a shirt against Igi. "Not one rip and every button intact."

That night Viv wrote to Edith Reesnes. Edith was a friend

from Deaconess Hospital days and the wife of the pastor whose church had sent the boxes. In the letter Viv said, "Lil is having a clothes sale tomorrow, right after breakfast. School starts Monday, so we are busy handing out toothbrushes and outfitting the girls and boys in clothes so they can go to school to learn to read and write. These children might be the future means of spreading the Word of God to their own people. They are poor people with no worldly riches, and so it is an extra pleasure to send word that there are clothes at our house for them. You send such good things, never a button missing or a seam open...."

She went on to add, "Lil, who is always in the middle of doing something, is a master at organizing a clothes sale and, best of all, she enjoys it. She charges twenty-five centavos for each item, about four American pennies, and a little more for adult clothes, to give the Tboli the self-respect that comes from buying something on their own. The money promptly goes into the literacy fund."

The next day, in the middle of the sale, a wrinkled old man approached Lil. He removed his shabby straw hat, then asked, "Do you have any clothes for a baby? My daughter is expecting her first child, and we don't have a cloth to wrap it in." His timeworn face creased into a smile when Lil picked out a blanket and tiny baby shirt for him.

"Keep them for me," he said anxiously. "I will come back in a few days with my twenty-five centavos." He watched intently while Lil wrote his name on a piece of paper and pinned it to the blanket. Then the old man adjusted his straw hat to shade his eyes and shuffled off toward the cornfields.

The Tboli on their way to and from market stopped by the house to scrutinize the rapidly diminishing clothes pile. Among them was Sem, Igi's little brother, grinning from ear to ear as he selected a pair of short, striped pants. Lil added a blue polo shirt to go with it. Now Sem could go to school, too.

Shortly before noon, after every scrap of clothing was gone, Lil gave each of the boys a box of crayons from the churches at Scandinavia and Farmington—their reward for all the times they had carried boxes home from the post office.

During those days, horseback riding, volleyball, climbing trees, and breaking bones were as much a part of life in the household at Sinolon as homework, plowing the cornfields, Bible studies, and singing. One afternoon, while the older boys cut off the branches of an old, dead tree, Dusin, the second-grader in the family, said, "Lift me up so I can cut off a branch."

The older boys refused. "You'd likely fall," they told him.

Dusin stayed close by, his eyes wistfully on the treetop. Finally, when the others dragged their branches to the back yard to be chopped for firewood, Dusin scampered up the tree without any help from anyone. Ten or fifteen feet in the air, he balanced precariously on a small branch, pulled his bolo out, and began whacking at a dead limb. When it fell, it snagged the branch on which Dusin wobbled. He tumbled down with the branches, still clutching his bolo. There was a piercing crash.

Those on the porch turned in time to see Dusin hit the ground. He scrambled up at once and started running toward the house, holding his arm as he ran. Halfway there, he crumpled.

When Viv and Lil reached him, it was obvious that he needed medical attention. "Your arm's broken," Viv said softly, her forehead wrinkling in concern.

Lil nodded. "Broken," she agreed.

Viv sat close to Dusin on the bumpy ride to Surala by cowsled and jeepney. He clutched his arm, dots of perspiration forming on his upper lip. When they reached Surala, he followed Vivian into the clinic, his dark eyes wide, troubled.

After examining Dusin, the Visayan doctor turned to

Vivian. "You'll have to go to Marbel and buy some plaster of Paris for casting. We'll put the boy's cast on this afternoon when you get back," he told her matter-of-factly.

Viv was stunned. Marbel was two hours away by public transportation. She walked out the door of the clinic without saying a word to Dusin, wondering to herself if there might be some place right in Surala to find the needed item. Dusin remained quietly on the bench, his arm wrapped in a coloring book, his lower lip trembling. When the door closed behind Vivian, he looked up at the doctor. He didn't know at all what Visayan doctors did with broken arms.

Meanwhile, Viv rushed from store to store, past the stalks of bananas, the barrels of dried fish, and the worn bins of rice. In the last place she checked in Surala, the lady had some Johnson and Johnson one-inch plaster of Paris strips, old as the hills around them. Viv quickly made her purchase, then hurried back to the hospital, arriving a little over an hour after she had left.

Not until Dusin awakened from the sodium pentothal did he tell Viv what had happened while she was gone. "A man took away the coloring-book sling and made me lie down on a table," Dusin whispered. "Then, without a word, he swung a big black x-ray machine over my arm. I was sure that the man was going to straighten my arm by putting that heavy machine on top of it. I was never so afraid in all my life." It was the only time Dusin cried through the whole ordeal. He looked away from Viv, then back. "Why did you leave me without a word, Little Mother?" he asked. "Where did you go?"

"They sent me to buy this." She tapped the damp cast that supported his arm.

"Na!" came the Tboli exclamation of surprise. "So that's why you left me?" Then he looked up from his cast and grinned at Viv. It was time to go home again.

Viv, too, was beginning to think in terms of going home;

not home to Sinolon, but to Everett, Washington. It was time for her third furlough, time to be with her family once more.

When she reached Everett, her brother Veryln had a brand new Vega waiting for her with fifty miles registered on the odometer. By the end of the year's furlough, when she turned the automobile back to her brother, Viv had covered 19,000 miles visiting friends, speaking in churches, acqainting others with the work of Bible translation—and best of all, she had shared many of those miles with her widowed mother.

Returning to the Philippines from furlough in the fall of 1973, Typhoon Ruth and the *S.S. Washington*, with Vivian on board, hit Manila about the same time. Viv was ready to begin her fourth term in the Islands.

The most exciting part about getting back to the house at Sinolon was meeting Nga To', the newest member of the family. Nga To' was Dusin's younger brother, bright and ambitious and as sparkly eyed as all the boys before him. Viv didn't know it then, but To' would be the last boy to join their family.

The goal on Viv's return from furlough was still the same—reaching the mountain people with God's Word in Tboli. Near her was a good reminder of the urgency of reaching others with God's Good News. At the edge of the yard, weeds crowded two gravesites. One belonged to a seventeen-year-old girl. While under treatment for malaria, the girl had died in their home—an unbeliever in the house full of believers. They had buried her in their yard and planted a branch on the top of the girl's grave, a tree to remind them that guests in their home must hear the name of Jesus. Next to her was the grave of a three-year-old. Bet had made a marker for the child's grave saying, *Dyuni—he arrived in God's country on July 16th.* At the beginning of this fourth term, Viv determined once again that with God's enabling there would be many Tboli whose hearts would be prepared to arrive in God's country.

Viv was quickly back into translation with Gadu, busily translating six new songs she had learned on furlough. They sang them morning, noon, and night—worshipful songs, sparkling and alive—songs the boys could sing as they crossed the river or worked the cornfields or taught on Sunday. These songs would encourage believers in the area, even with the growing unrest on Mindanao. The words would continue to echo in the valley long after Viv and Marge's evacuation from Sinolon to Nasuli a year later.

There were other sounds echoing in the valley, too. The weekly Christian radio broadcasts in Tboli and Gospel Recordings cassette tapes and records were taking the message of reconciliation to thousands of illiterate Tboli scattered throughout the mountains. These media were reaching higher into the mountains than the translation team could ever climb.

In the first venture with Gospel Recordings, the hymns and the dialogue of Christ's parables spoke right back to the people as they played the "Tboli plates." Many of the families determined then and there to have one of those record machines and settled among themselves what the price would be. "Just think, Little Mother," commented one Tboli, "only a sack and a half of rice for such a machine."

The Tboli themselves were also carrying the message of God's love. Faw, a young Tboli teen-ager, accompanied Secretary Elizalde on a visit to the isolated Tasaday people. While there, Faw asked the people if they knew God. The Tasaday answered, "We don't know him. There's been no one to tell us."

Faw made up for lost time, telling them about Jesus, about his love. "They continually listened, Little Mother," Faw told Vivian later. "They learned the songs very quickly. I was constantly singing to them. Sir Elizalde was there, and he liked our songs in Tboli. I said, 'Sir, we are singing about our God, the One who is in the highest, who long ago created the earth and the sky and every single thing on the earth.' "

Faw's dark eyes were round with excitement as she told her story. And then a look of puzzlement crossed her face. "When I told Sir that, he would only nod. He didn't speak." Then she went on. "When I left the Tasaday, it was already six nights that I was there. I said to them, 'God will take care of you.' But it was just words into the air," Faw explained. "They could not understand it."

But Viv knew that a seed had been planted; a song had been sung.

In a totally different direction from the Tasaday, two young Peace Corps members hiked up to Mt. Parker, a volcanic area in the jungles, in the middle of nowhere. There were no roads, few tourists.

In passing through Sinolon on their return, Dick, the taller of the two hikers, said to the translators, "We ran into one of your churches up there."

"One of our churches?" Doris exclaimed. "What do you mean, one of our churches?"

"Well," Dick answered, "The Tboli said it was your church. And they were singing your songs and using your songbooks."

Doris brightened. As the result of literacy classes another little church had no doubt sprung up, completely indigenous. Perhaps it was one more missionary outreach from Muto Got, the church at the mountaintop.

26
CHURCH AT THE MOUNTAINTOP

The church at Muto Got lay across the Sefali River, up a steep climb, down into a deep gorge, then up, up, up again to the top of the next range. For years Muto Got was far beyond the reach of the Tboli team. They could make it to the top of some of the smaller hills, Lil with her walking stick and Gadu mimicking her all the way. But the people at Muto Got were thoroughly scattered, with a mountain or valley between every home.

Finally Gadu said, "I'm going up to Muto Got and see whether any of the people would like a teacher to come on Sundays." He went, traveling the broad distance from home to home, asking if they would like a church.

"Yes," the people replied.

"If you really want someone to teach you, then gather up the materials and start putting up a building," Gadu instructed.

By the following weekend he found the church building going up. Men, their shoulders red and swollen from carrying support posts, were finishing a roof of split bamboo laid like tiles. Inside the building, rattan-tied bamboo benches sat row upon row on a dirt floor. All that had been necessary to build this little church was bamboo, a dollar and fifty cents worth of nails, cooperation, and the faith of Gadu. In time the little building would become "a house for calling on

167

God" on Sundays; "a house for learning to read" on week-days.

Every week Gadu went off to Muto Got, armed with a message from Tboli Scriptures. Neither going up nor coming down was easy for the translators who had begun following him to the mountain peak. Once they reached the summit, they could understand why Tboli built on mountaintops. It was beautiful. The sky seemed within hand's reach, the air clean and refreshing. The view down the slopes was breathtaking, a splendor of color, with the entire Tboli world at their fingertips.

But the real church at the mountaintop was made of people. On Sunday, the translators watched them come, a hundred or more men and women, boys and girls coming long distances to meet together.

The men took their seats on one side of the church. The women walked to the front and left their baskets—filling the altar with corn, sweet potatoes, beans, eggplants, onions, ginger, herbs, bananas—the very best of what they had as an offering to God.

Everyone took part reviewing the lesson of the previous Sunday. Only the dogs, as regular in their attendance as their owners, slept through the service. After the review, Gadu taught the new lesson, gently sharing the truths he had learned at the translation desk with Viv and Doris. "This does not come from my own thinking," he said to the older people. "But it is what I have learned from God's Word." Again there was audience participation—comments, questions, discussions, exclamations.

One old woman stood and said, "Are people asking to see the power of God? Then tell them to look at me. Formerly I was always sick, never able to work regularly. Now is there a day you don't see me working, providing food for my family? That's God's power. And I'm no longer chewing betelnut. Could an old woman like me give up chewing betelnut except for God's power? I am eating many foods—would I dare to break a taboo but for God's power to help me? As for my sins, God was able to remove them all and give me a peaceful breath. Is not this the power of God?"

A short distance from the church, the children sat on huge logs at the edge of a clearing. Banana leaves and palm fronds shaded their little cove. Colorful orchids and flamboyant flowers were everywhere. Min sat facing the girls and boys, reciting a chapter from *Little Pilgrim's Progress,* helping the children memorize songs and Bible verses. Then they prayed together. "Help me so I won't forget the story," one little boy prayed. "Then it will be right when I tell others." This was Sunday school, Tboli style.

For Viv, the exhausting mountain climb and the restricted diet faded into insignificance as she saw Tboli people responding to God's love. She could see it in their eyes, their faces, and their spontaneous reactions. But for every Tboli who experienced peace with God, there were still hundreds who had never heard the name of Jesus. Others had heard but weren't interested. Of some of the older people the boys would say, "Their thinking is short. God's Word hasn't reached them yet."

Viv knew that attending regular church services in a designated building and heeding the teachings of a younger man were not cultural for the Tboli. In the early days, church was held in homes, where the older men could lie back on their mats, pretending not to listen, yet hearing without the humiliation of openly submitting to the instruction of younger men. The fact that Jesus could free them from the power of evil spirits attracted Tboli to Jesus. In many instances, recognition of freedom from sin came later, after they had accepted Christ.

Christianity had proved practical within the culture. Lowlanders generally placed the mountain people at the bottom

of the social scale. But for the Tboli, knowing Christ—
knowing that Jesus died for them, had a purpose for them,
wanted them—made a great change in their attitude about
themselves. It gave them new courage to stand up for their
rights against the lowlanders. Tboli custom required them to
help out in the family unit, but they were not obligated to
help a friend or a neighbor. Now believers at Muto Got and
other Tboli churches in the mountains were stepping in
willingly to help one another in times of sickness and death.
All over the mountains God's Word was taking root, faith for
the mountain people coming by hearing and hearing by the
Word of God in Tboli.

Ma' Bita', the father of Bita', was one of the oldest men in
Muto Got to become a follower of God. "When Gadu
taught in our place, that's when my thinking changed . . .
that's what brought me to God," he declared.

Although suffering from tuberculosis, Ma' Bita' was determined to learn to read, motivated by his deep desire to
know the Scriptures. He hiked the mountain trails three
hours a day, rain or shine, to attend literacy classes in Datal
Tedblow, arriving in his ragged shirt and pants. During a full
morning of literacy classes, he'd dig his bare toes into the dirt
floor and squint intently as the phonetic symbols formed
together into words and Tboli thought patterns.

One morning in the middle of the literacy campaign Ma'
Bita' lingered after class, his book tucked into his shirt. His
bolo swung freely at his side as he twirled his knobbed hat
awkwardly in one hand. "Is it all right if I am absent tomorrow?" he asked the translators. "I need to work to earn a
little money to buy some soap and salt."

God's Word was coming at great cost to this Tboli man.
He was breaking cultural patterns to study with younger
men; climbing steep mountain trails when his health was
poor; working overtime in his cornfield to meet the needs of
his family.

There were several youths from Muto Got who learned to read at the same time as Ma' Bita'. Kas, ambitious and competitive; Unus, four feet, ten inches of energy and enthusiasm; and Minda, Pilar, and Wat—all young and capable.

After the literacy campaign was over, Ma' Bita' spent all his spare time reading books of Scripture. Later, he wrote to Gadu, "All that is in my breath these days is to tell God's Word to others."

When Gadu moved on to another area to teach, the church at Muto Got was left in the care of Ma' Bita.' As time passed, Ma' Bita' became more and more burdened for people in other areas where there was no instruction.

"What are we going to do to reach these people?" he asked the other believers. He turned to the young men in his church and said, "Kas, you go. Unus, you go. And Wat, you go. Teach others."

They caught Ma' Bita's vision and began taking the Word of God to distant places. Because of this effort, the Word of God in Tboli, sharper than any two-edged sword, began making deep inroads into hearts and lives. Little churches began popping up in areas where the translators had never been.

While the firsthand exposure to God's Word was changing lives, challenging them, the conflicts over the land between Muslims and lowlanders were spreading throughout the province of Cotabato. Revenge killings among rebel insurgents were on the increase. Zamboanga, a southern city on Mindanao—and according to the newspapers "a city on the edge of civil war"—was swarming with government troops and refugees from other areas.

Two years before, on 23 September 1972, President Marcos had declared martial law in the country of the Philippines. Martial law was reimposed by the president in January 1973, bringing with it an even greater measure of peace and control within the country. But his action had not completely stilled the rebel uprisings on Mindanao or silenced the rumors of unrest. Small skirmishes subsided in one area, only to break out in another. Nevertheless, in spite of the rumors of war, Gadu had continued to carry the Good News in Tboli to the mountaintop at Muto Got, and the church at Muto Got continued its missionary outreach from mountain range to mountain range.

Back at Sinolon, Vivian and Igi were washing dishes one Sunday evening while Marge tuned in a radio broadcast. Again the news was disturbing. Immediately, sixteen-year-old Igi—their boy with the thick, curly eyelashes—turned toward Viv, his dishtowel still making circular motions on the plate he was drying. When he spoke, his deep voice was earnest. "Be sure to tell us ahead of time, Little Mother, if a real war comes so that I can pocket the book of Timothy. Wherever I go, it goes with me."

Viv felt like singing. The Word of God was becoming necessary to a Tboli.

The rumor of unrest was not the only problem. Many of the people had lost their corn crops and their year's rice harvest to the grasshoppers and rats. The grasshoppers came one August afternoon like a thick, ominous cloud, circling several times, then settling down on the boys' unharvested cornfield next to the airstrip. All night long the field was crowded with Tboli, catching the grasshoppers by the sackful to eat and sell in the market the next day. The household at Sinolon was out with the rest, filling their sacks and eating grasshoppers, too; Snoopy, the boys' wheat-colored German shepherd, stayed right at their heels.

In spite of the rats, the grasshoppers, and the threat of unrest in the area, September 1974 was a red-letter month for the Tboli believers. Many were to be baptized at four major teaching areas during September, one group each Sunday. At each place the Lord's Supper was to be observed for the first time. Instead of bread and wine, which were nonexistent in the culture, the Tboli used what they served at an ordinary meal. "For this is really what Jesus did," Walan explained. And so Walan, Bedung, and Gadu passed the sweet potato and water, quietly asking their own people in each area to "do this in remembrance of the Lord who loved Tboli, too."

None of the team members had pushed the ordinances of baptism or communion on the people. The Tboli, like the Ethiopian eunuch talking to Philip, had asked, "What hinders us from being baptized?" And like Philip, the team had answered, "Nothing, if you believe in Jesus with all your heart."

Likewise, it had been the Scriptures themselves that taught the people about the Lord's Supper. Walan had been studying Corinthians and felt that the communion ordinance should also be part of Tboli worship.

On the week they met at Bedung's church, twenty-three Tboli, including Igi's mother and Dusin, followed the Lord in the waters of baptism. An overflowing crowd filled the little church. Babies were hanging in their cloth hammocks from the rafters. Big black cooking pots filled with rice for the noon meal also hung from the rafters. A bundle of cassava and vegetables and a pile of leaves for plates had been stacked near the end of one bench.

The highlight of the day for Walan was when his wife, Umek, the mother of his four children, quit her struggle against faith and said simply, "I've been so jealous . . . but now I want to follow Jesus."

In the quiet beauty of that day, God was preparing his people to trust him in a new way. Only hours away—off to the east—the rebel insurgents were moving in, looting and burning. The morning after Umek followed Jesus, threats of turbulence in the area loomed closer to Sinolon than the team dreamed possible. The Visayans evacuated immedi-

ately. One week later, on 15 September 1974, Viv and
Marge, who had never been quick to run when the going got
tough, were evacuated from the barrio of Sinolon to the
Wycliffe center at Nasuli as a precautionary measure. Their
evacuation, unbeknown to them, closed the door to a way
of life in a bamboo house that had so often been bursting
with boys and laughter.

27

BARRELS ARE
FOR PACKING

Through the years, people at home—friends and prayer supporters in Canada and the United States—had shared in the mountain-climbing experience of giving God's Word to the Tboli. All along they had been part of the team. When news reached them that Viv and Marge had been evacuated from Sinolon, they kept praying. Because of their faith and encouragement, three of the translators—Vivian, Marge and Lil—were able to move back to Sinolon in March 1975, six months after the evacuation.

Although other areas suffered damage and a few Tboli died in rebel skirmishes, there had been no looting, burning, or stealing in Sinolon. Still, as a defensive measure, hundreds of Tboli men had been trained in the local barrio self-defense units; Gadu, Tunyu, and Mai served as leaders for three of the smaller units. For the most part these Tboli soldiers were just teen-agers, young men unskilled and untrained in the arts of warfare. Because some had already been killed, Gadu and his unit memorized Psalm 91 and other Scripture portions to steady them in the continuing conflict.

When the translators returned to Sinolon, they settled temporarily in Ethel Moorehouse's home. Viv stood alone in her desire to repair the isolated house in the gully. It was stripped bare, its thatched roof rotted, the airstrip overgrown with weeds, and all the boys had long since scattered. Min, Dusin, and Nga To', the younger boys, and Kasi the stutterer were living across the river near Bedung. Fa and Tunyu had both married. Igi, their high-schooler, was eager to return to King's Institute to complete his schooling. And Mai was still mayor at Kemotu.

Finally Viv had to admit it. The evacuation from Sinolon and the political unrest had been the means of bringing their household of boys to an end. It was not the time to build again, to gather in supplies, to rear Tboli children. The original goal was the main one now. Finish the New Testament. See it safely into the hands of the people. Then, no matter what happened, God's Word would work its own miracles.

For the translators, that first Saturday back in the Alah Valley was the usual wild market day, the team wading knee-deep in necklaces and medicines. The next day they hiked to Bedung's church across the Sefali River. The new thatched building with open walls was three times as big as the old one. Backless benches lined both sides of the room, a room overflowing with one hundred fifty Tboli. Women and children sat on one side, men on the other. Scripture portions and hymnbooks lay open on the laps of many believers. But there was a new feature. *Guns rested upright on the ground beside the men,* shouting the silent message that uncertainty still reigned in the valley, and rumors were still spreading. It gave Viv and the team a new sense of urgency to get the New Testament completed so more Tboli could pocket God's Word in their hearts for the unsettled days ahead.

Gadu and Bedung were both available for translation. And Selanting, still struggling spiritually and considering a second wife, shyly, hesitantly talked again about leaving PANAMIN and giving his time to translation until the work on the Tboli New Testament was done. His offer was far above the girls' wildest dreams. They wondered, Was God reminding Ting of the promise he had made on the night of his mother's death? Viv and the others were confident that God would keep his part of the bargain. He would continue to remind Selanting of the promises he had made. What Ting did with God's wooing would be a personal matter. Yet even in the face of the urgency to finish the work, the translators had to wait in the unhurried pace of the people for Ting's final decision.

The last New Testament book to be translated was Hebrews, the same book Viv had been reading when she committed herself to the Lord to go anywhere, to be anything. For Viv the theme of Hebrews came through loud and clear. In one of the manuscripts she checked for another translation team, the word *covenant* had been translated as "the way God prepared for man to approach him."

Viv was eager to finish the translation task, perhaps with Selanting, perhaps with Gadu—eager to tell the way God had prepared for Tboli to approach him. At one of the recent workshops Myra Lou Barnard and Jan Forster had submitted their own finished translation. Myra Lou, the Wycliffe colleague who had been so severely burned and had so influenced Viv during her first term in the Philippines, completed her part of the Dibabawon New Testament sitting in a hammock with her scarred legs elevated. The Dibabawon New Testament challenged Viv. She tackled her own assignment with fresh enthusiasm, even though she knew there would be other lessons ahead, other obstacles to hurdle, before the Tboli New Testament rolled through the Marshburn Press in Manila.

In April 1975, on the Thursday before Easter, three weeks after the team returned to Sinolon, a cablegram message from Everett, Washington, reached Nasuli. Ed Ruch, associate director at the center, relayed its contents on the morning radio schedule. As kindly as he could, he said, "Viv, you'll have to pack for home. Your mom is critically ill, dying."

Within an hour the JAARS pilot reached Sinolon and was winging Viv to Cagayan de Oro for the nearest phone connection to the United States. Good Friday in the Philippines was a holy day, with no commercial flights available, but Viv would be on her way home by Saturday.

Immediately the Philippine branch members, a sharing, closely knit group, rallied in support. As one friend handed her a check for thirty dollars, Viv looked at it, too stunned to reply. Ann broke the silence, saying, "It's okay, Viv. The check is good."

At the same time Viv's personal crisis came, the Wycliffe SIL branch in Vietnam was also packing. SILers there had remained in the country throughout the Viet conflict. But in the face of the 1975 North Vietnamese advance into South Vietnam, and with one Wycliffe couple and their small daughter already in captivity,* there was no choice for SIL but to withdraw. Many of the Vietnam translation teams were flying directly to the Philippines and relocating there.

Saturday, as Vivian waited in Cagayan de Oro to board the commercial flight for Manila, the first planeload of Bible translators, Vietnam evacuees, was transferring for the flight to Nasuli. The urgency of finishing a translation magnified itself in the faces of these colleagues. There was no guarantee of time, not with the fall of Cambodia and Vietnam.

Two needs were clearly etched in Vivian's mind as she made her lonely journey to the States: the uprooting of her colleagues from Vietnam, and her mom. Vivian had often asked the Lord for the privilege of being with her mother when she received her call into eternity. Thanks to the work of Viv's directors, the pilots, and the government man in

*John and Carolyn Miller and daughter were released in October 1975.

Manila, she arrived at her mother's bedside on Easter Sunday, a few hours before her younger sister Phyllis flew in from Minnesota.

Surprisingly, the hours in the critical care unit proved the onset of a happy family reunion. The Forsbergs could not be together long without reminiscing, laughing, and enjoying one another's presence. It was the tonic that Winnie Forsberg needed. In spite of the blockage of cerebral arteries and the complication of pneumonia, Viv's mom began to recover. But she would never be physically strong enough to live alone.

Now Viv found herself encountering a completely unexpected problem. Should she remain at home with her mother? If she stayed in Everett, there would be no need to close up the apartment and move her mother to the Bethany Home. Suddenly for Vivian the cost of the Tboli New Testament demanded digging at deep, personal roots.

It was Winnie Forsberg herself who made the decision clear. "Vivian just has to get back to the Philippines and finish that translation." Like the parents of the other team members, Viv's mom had been a part of the Tboli team for a long time. She wasn't pulling out now.

After all, Winnie Forsberg had a stake in the Tboli New Testament. Five hundred dollars of her life's savings had been the start of a bank account for the publishing of the completed New Testament. With the soaring printing costs in Manila, the World Home Bible League estimated that five thousand copies of the Tboli New Testament would run ten thousand dollars or more. The price was staggering and rising, but like the widow's mite, Winnie Forsberg's gift had been given in love and was sure to multiply.

Bethany Home, where Mrs. Forsberg would move, was a four-story Lutheran facility on Broadway, one of the main streets in downtown Everett. The senior citizens at Bethany had been a part of the Tboli team ever since Vivian worked there during her second furlough. They had little left to give but their love and their prayers, but these they gave whole-heartedly. Viv was confident that there were rooms in this building where the Lord came to be refreshed, just as he did in the Bethany of old.

"I feel so safe leaving prayer requests with you," she said one evening as she talked to the white-haired congregation at Bethany. "Every time we sit down to a meal, let's pray for the missionary captives in Vietnam. And when we crawl into our beds tonight, let's pray for them."

Grandma Moen, nigh to ninety and spry as a cricket, nodded in agreement. From then on, whenever Viv was on her way to the fourth floor to visit her own mother, Bethany residents stopped her in the hallway to say, "We just can't eat now without remembering to pray."

Across the country, in Wisconsin, others were praying. All four of the translation team were well acquainted with Art and Edith Reesnes and their two-point American Lutheran parish in the farming communities of Scandinavia and Farmington. Edith and Art, who had once been Viv's pastor, grew up in homes where missionaries were loved and wel-comed. Shortly after the completion of one women's mis-sionary project at Scandinavia, the ladies of the parish asked, "Now what can we do?"

"I have a missionary friend in the Philippines, translating the Scriptures," Edith had answered. "Would you like me to write and ask her if there is something we can do to help?"

Several weeks later Edith shared Vivian's answer with the women's groups at both churches—the request for used clothing for Tboli children. In the days that followed, the clothes just started coming in. No matter how often the church mailed the boxes to Tboli land, when the women met again and opened the "Philippine closet," there were more shopping bags, boxes, and bundles with clothes for the Tboli.

In Everett, as Viv packed for her return to the translation work, she was reminded of what Wycliffe translator Julia Supple had once said, "Fellow translators, let me say that if you're on the home stretch to finish the *Book*, cover your daily lives with the blood of Jesus. You'll need it. And to the small prayer groups that have stood behind us, let me say, *you have made the difference.*"

Viv agreed. The Tboli team had praying friends across the country, friends like those at Bethany and those from Scandinavia and Farmington. They had made the difference.

Always before in preparing to leave for the Philippines, Viv had been caught up in the business of packing barrels—big, black, fifty-gallon barrels. It had been part of missionary living. She and the team had packed and unpacked these huge drums every time they prepared for furlough and every time they returned to the field. Viv's own first fifty-gallon barrels, with every bit of space packed full, went over the roadless countryside to Sinolon in 1953. Memories of friends and loved ones were tucked in those barrels and unraveled as she unpacked tools and towels, bed linens and clothing. Once unpacked, the barrels served readily as storage space or water tanks, perched high on platforms to catch rain for the daily water supply.

Barrels and crates brim-filled with hymnbooks, literacy materials, and printed portions of the Word of God were the first items evacuated when the rebel insurgents moved into the Alah Valley in the fall of 1974. There were other items that the team could never pack into barrels—memories of twenty years or more of living with the Tboli people and warm thoughts of people at home who had cared for the Tboli.

This time Viv packed lightly, carefully tucking the essentials into two suitcases. She was limited by the restrictions on international flights, limited by these uncertain times in village living. Packing was difficult, frustrating. She disliked the job intensely. But as far as Viv was concerned, the hardest part of all missionary work was just ahead—saying good-bye again to her own family.

On 14 May 1975, Viv and Wycliffe colleague Hazel Wrigglesworth, a graceful young woman with a pervading aura of dignity, boarded a plane for the return trip to the Philippine Islands. At the airport, directly in front of the observation tower, their jet nosed skyward. As the plane disappeared like a speck in the gray cloud, winging her home to Sinolon, Viv was comforted, knowing there would be no packing in heaven. No good-byes.

Her work of Bible translation would not be finished until the Tboli mountain people had the complete New Testament in their hands and were taught to read it. She and the translation team were "on the home stretch to finish the *Book*." The end was in view.

28
THEY ARE
MY GLORY

Saturday evening, after a smooth flight halfway around the world, their jet touched down in Manila. Vivian and Hazel, weighted down with typewriters and Hazel's heavy cosmetic bag, stepped off the plane into the oppressive Manila heat. They were both convinced, as they saw the beautiful, familiar Filipino faces, that reaching others, especially tribal folk on Mindanao, was high priority on God's list of things to be done before he sent his Son back to earth. Both women were eager to get back to translation. In fact, there was nothing Viv enjoyed more.

Of course, over the years, giving God's Word to the Tboli had had its problems. More than once God had tested the foundation on which the team stood, reminding them in his own special way that it would cost them something to give the Tboli the Word of God in their own language. The stakes proved high when the village of Kemotu sprang up. It twirled the team around, shook them up. Had God pulled in the reins, they wondered? Had he allowed PANAMIN? Had he magnified the cultural shock after all those years on the field just to show them he loved them, wanted them completely? Their time? Their efforts? Their desires? Whatever the reason, God would be glorified, the team strengthened, the Tboli church leadership purified.

For Viv, Isaiah was still ringing loud and clear, "Sing, O

barren, thou that didst not bear; break forth into singing . . .
enlarge the place of thy tent . . . spare not . . . strengthen thy
stakes" (Isaiah 54:1-2, KJV). As she headed south to Mindanao she knew she loved translation. But this time she
loved the Lord Jesus more.

By July 1976 Gadu, their chief translation helper, was
appearing irregularly for the final revision of the translation,
dividing his time haphazardly between the PANAMIN clinic
and the barrio school that would give him a high school
diploma for attending occasionally. Mai had taken on wife
number seven. Two of the younger men who had once lived
in their household were drinking heavily. Doris, Marge, and
Lil continued to do research in order to feed Viv the needed
information as the revision continued; but sometimes it
seemed that they were pushing and scolding "to get things
done."

Then one evening Mai, Ting, and Fludi came to Ethel's
house to visit Viv and Lil. It was long after midnight before
they stood to leave. "When do you plan to go to Nasuli?"
Mai asked from the doorway.

"Not until the New Testament is finished," Viv told him
firmly.

Mai rubbed his right hand against his straggly beard. He
watched her with a troubled gaze. "Go by September," he
urged.

"Why?" Viv eyed him curiously. Mai, who had always
gone with the current, seemed concerned.

"Because of the fighting. From all the official sources
there will be more fighting in the area by September. We will
counterattack."

"You could help us finish," Viv ventured.

He smiled crookedly, averting his eyes. "It's too late
now," he said.

That Sunday, during the morning service in a nearby
barrio, one old Tboli man stood to speak. As he closed his

testimony he said, "And that is why I absolutely refused to sign the petition to drive the Americans out of here. I would never sign that paper. No matter what they might do to me, I would never sign."

For a moment Viv thought he referred to a recent political effort to remove a Catholic mission from the area. But as the old man continued to speak, Viv stiffened; her insides turned sour. It was obviously a petition to remove the Tboli team.

"All Americans will be asked to leave the Philippines," the man concluded.

Had the man misunderstood the rumors? Viv could not be sure. That afternoon she went to her study in Ethel's house. It was quiet outside, but an unsettled quietness. She sat alone except for seven motherless chicks, one lame duckling, and Ethel's dog, Prince, at her feet. She turned to the book of Hebrews, chapter eleven. As she read of the men of faith who had heard the promises but had not seen them or touched them, she paused. *Funny,* she thought, *when you step out in obedience to God—he doesn't smile because of your high aspirations. God knows they aren't nearly high enough. He is going to do far greater than any of our expectations. But he doesn't promise that we'll see the results,* she reflected.

God had never promised her an easy journey. After all, God's breakthrough to the Tboli came by individuals. One here. One there—seemingly scattered but perfectly planned by God. Now, Tboli—barefoot and muscular—were pounding the dirt trails to reach others, drawing their strength from the Lord.

As she thought further, it boiled down to what 1 Corinthians said. God was picking up the weak vessels in Tboli country, too. Walan, the plodder; Gadu, the bouncy Peter Rabbit; Ma' Bita', sick with tuberculosis; and Wat, Kas, Unus, Fining, and Faw—Tboli who felt the burden to take

the Scriptures to their own people. The translation team
provided Scripture portions. But the *Holy Spirit* worked in
the hearts and lives of the Tboli people.

In the translation of the gospel of John, one verse stood
out. The Lord Jesus had said of the men and women who
followed Him, "They are my glory" (John 17:10, LB).
Young men like Gadu, Walan, and Bedung. Old men like
the grandfather of Dusin and the father of Igi.

Walan, short and chubby and the father of four children,
was the oldest boy from the household at Sinolon. He was
the first Tboli to hike down the mountainside to school, the
first to graduate from high school. Gentle and deliberate,
Walan had never been energetic like Yadan, or political like
Mai. But for nineteen years, he had faithfully tramped the
mountain trails, encouraging his own people to believe
God's Good News.

Though still young, Walan suffered for months from
rheumatoid arthritis. For a time he could hardly limp to his
own fields in the morning or bend his knees. Trails were
difficult. The more he knew God, the more simply he
prayed about the pain. As his prayers multiplied, the arthritis
completely left him.

In the little church where Walan had taught all these
years, he was happy to have thirty adults in attendance. By
December 1977 over one hundred Tboli filled the church
service every Sunday morning. Men who had been involved up to their necks in Kemotu were confessing their
sins, making new commitments to God.

"We can't afford to pay a pastor or a literacy teacher,"
they told Walan as they handed him vegetables and
bananas for his family. Back at Sinolon, Walan stopped to
see Viv and Lil, his eyes shining, a smile spreading across his
sharp cheekbones. "It is easy to open up a conversation
about Jesus with those cassette players," he said. And then

he added, "We really need literacy. But in all these things, if we are going to succeed, we're going to have to have the presence of the Lord with us."

Gadu—younger than Walan, a dreamer, a singer, a poet of sorts like his dad—had become a follower of God at the age of twelve. As a grown young man, a bit taller than most Tboli, Gadu still merrily contributed his laughter whenever he was around. But he was also fiery, explosive. After Mai left the translation work, Gadu took to Bible translation like a carabao takes to a cool, muddy stream. He seemed to feel a responsibility to complete the Tboli New Testament. Because of this conviction, he stayed away from the early attractions of PANAMIN.

After the team evacuated Sinolon, Gadu periodically sought employment in Kemotu as a means of supporting his widowed mother and younger brothers. Many months later, the team realized that money for Gadu had led to a new temptation—gambling, betting. They did not approve, but it was not their responsibility to force their convictions on the Tboli church. They would have to trust God to convict, challenge, change, and direct his individual followers.

Bedung, another of the young men from the translators' home, was responsible for the church an hour from the house in the gully. Shy and stocky, short for a Tboli, Bedung never would have been picked by the team to be a pastor. Now he preached regularly and more and more was taking over as literacy supervisor. Because of his steadiness, his dependability, one team member said, "I wish we had ten more like him." And another added, "We got a jewel when we got Bedung—the Scriptures have taken control of his life."

When PANAMIN came, Bedung was content to live near the church at the foot of the mountains, happy with what he had, happy with his wife, Inuk, and their child, Imi. He made

no attempt to cash in on the material benefits in the new
barrio of Kemotu. His concern for his own people kept him
in the Gospel ministry.

The father of Bedung—the grandfather of Dusin—was
the oldest Tboli attending Bedung's church. Bedung's father
could no longer work the cornfields. He and his only wife,
the mother of his eleven children, lived at the foot of the
mountains in a typical bamboo home with four walls, a
sleeping mat, a fire table, three cooking pots, and a bamboo
section for carrying water.

He stood, slightly stooped from the loads carried over the
years, wearing a black sweatshirt from the missionary
barrel—a very old man with a lined face, work-hardened
hands, and a dignity about him that demanded respect. His
feet were thickly calloused, his toes widespread from walking the mountains. But when he bowed his gray, curly head
and talked to God in a soft-spoken voice, Tboli listened.
People still walked three mountains to hear him pray.

Years before, Selanting had written to Vivian, "One Sunday night I slept in the mountains at the Father of Bedung's—the Grandfather of Dusin. I was unable to return
home because of hard rain. Very strong is the faith in that
home. I could never win over them in praying. After we had
all laid down to sleep, a child who was sick became deliri-
ous. Then I heard the Father of Bedung pray. Little Mother,
in that one I have really seen an old man among the Tboli
who has truly changed, who has become a new man altogether."

In recent years another man stood up in one of the
Sunday morning services and told of God's patience in
dealing with a people who started out with no knowledge of
God at all. Igi's father had been hearing God's Word for
some time, hearing and believing it but not obeying it.

That Sunday, with unrest still mounting in the Alah Valley,
he stood facing his own people, his skin taut against his high

cheekbones. He ran his fingers over his forehead, pushing his black, unruly hair into place. Then he spoke. "Already twelve years now I've been hearing the Word of God. And for one who doesn't know how to read, hearing the Word of God is like the light rain falling on one. It takes a long time to get wet. That's the way it has been, my hearing the Word of God. It's taken me all these years to understand what God did for me through Jesus Christ, and what it means to follow and obey him."

29

THE TURNING
OF THE PAGES

In January 1977, at the director's request, the translation team moved back to the Wycliffe center to spend longer hours at the revision, with fewer interruptions.

The study on the ground level at the missionaries' house at Nasuli was a large, screened-in room with glass-louver windows and Larry Walrod's sprawling, timeworn desk for Viv's working space. Gadu began his workday in the rocking chair across from Viv. "Little Mother," he said seriously after flipping from the rocking chair and somersaulting across the room, ending with a cartwheel, "This book must sound just like the old men who really know how to talk."

He was setting the standard for the Tboli New Testament—paying the highest compliment in the Tboli culture, where old men were revered.

As weeks and months of Tboli revision went on, Gadu's expressions often brought Viv up short. She had just finished reading a portion of 1 Corinthians when Gadu frowned. "Segton ko?—does it match?" He tapped his brown forefinger soundly against the stock of commentaries, the thick copy of *Jamieson, Faussett and Brown* on top.

"Is it exegetically correct?" she teased back. He had a right to know whether their Tboli translation actually conveyed what the New Testament writer had intended to say. It was a heavy responsibility for Viv. She would be earnest in checking the translations, the commentaries, and in seeking the Holy Spirit's guidance before she gave her final answer.

By mid-May Nasuli was hot, uncomfortable. Wilted, Gadu pulled off his shirt and tossed it in the corner. He sat, perspiring in short, khaki trousers, his bare feet resting on the rung of the rocker. But the atmosphere at the center was different, less threatening. There were minimal distractions.

On 22 May, they took time out to celebrate Igi's birthday. Igi, who had graduated from high school the month before, was spending a brief time at Nasuli, helping in the revision. Walan and Fa were there, too.

Earlier Gadu had asked Fa to come and be his companion at the center. Fa had refused. Still concerned about Fa's recent separation from his child-wife, Gadu invited him again in April. Fa responded, "I feel like I should come, but what of my job?"

Fa was working for Mai at Kemotu. Finally he asked Mai's permission. "Gadu wants me and our mothers want me to come and help on the New Testament," he explained. Mai did an about-face. He granted Fa permission to help for a month.

Now the downstairs rooms at the missionaries' house looked like a miniature Tboli workshop. Viv and Gadu worked alone in the study on 2 Corinthians. Lil settled at a desk in Marge's old downstairs bedroom, busily proofreading 1 Corinthians. Walan typed in another corner of the room, while Igi stretched out in the open area by the staircase, his bare legs catching the sunshine as he proofread a section of the Tboli Scriptures. Upstairs in the main part of the house, a visiting C&MA missionary worked at the dining-room table. Fa used the bodega, converted now into a study, quietly working on a rough draft of Proverbs. The words of Solomon on trust and obedience touched Fa in areas in his life where he most needed help.

While Fa was at Nasuli, the father and mother of Sima, an

older couple, believers who had learned to read and write only the year before, wrote to Fa, saying, "How great was our thankfulness to God when we heard that you had again returned to your former work. You haven't forgotten, have you, when you formerly taught God's Word among us? We'll help you now in our praying to God for you so that you will not again leave Jesus."

As far as Viv was concerned, God was working new miracles in Fa's life and attitudes. She wondered, Was there any reason to doubt that he would perform another miracle for Fa and his child-wife?

The work moved ahead when the others were there, but for the most part Viv and Gadu struggled alone in the revision. The others eventually returned to their homes and responsibilities at Sinolon and Kemotu, while Lil was called home to New York for a family emergency.

One morning during the final polish of the epistles, Gadu called out from the window where he seemed totally absorbed in the good weather and the scenery. "Tagad, Ye' Udi—Wait a minute, Little Mother," he demanded, whirling to face her. That was Gadu's signal. He wasn't quite satisfied that the translation was as good as they could make it.

On one occasion after discovering a correction herself, Viv said, "You know, Gadu, I was just thinking . . . we could really link these two verses together . . . or do you think we should leave them separate. . . ."

She looked up. Gadu remained silent, shaking his head in exasperation. "Teyem uu, Ye' Udi—Good grief, Little Mother. Don't just think, write. Write. I might lose this. Think afterwards. How can a person think with so much talking going on?"

He stared at Viv with dark, piercing eyes and said more politely, "This is correct; it doesn't need any changes." Immediately he proceeded to search for better Tboli terminology and came up with a better phrase.

In December it was stuffy in the study. A late afternoon

tropical storm battered the closed louver windows. Outside
it was raining bolos and hammer handles, turning the paths
in front of the house into a muddy, turbulent river. The
electric lights from the base generator flickered on and off.
Gadu dropped to the floor for a series of pushups. Then he
stood and stretched, his muscular arms bulging, his broad
hands and fingers flexing. "Pray, Little Mother," he said
softly. "It is as if Satan does not wish us to finish."

Viv nodded. It seemed to her, too, as if Satan had tried
everything to get Gadu sidetracked, but Gadu had remained committed to the completion of the translation even
though revision was upstream all the way. At times she and
Gadu had hit a slump, dragging their feet—their faith
threadbare. Often their personalities grated against each
other. Yet Viv marveled at what the Lord was doing, even on
the days when they limped through revision.

She marveled even more at what God was doing through
Gadu. If anyone had told her when Gadu came to their
household as a first-grader that down the line the two of
them would be revising the Tboli New Testament, she
would have laughed. Called them crazy. Not Gadu, their
star athlete—running, high jumping, tossing the basketball.
Lazy and irresponsible when it came to mundane household chores and plowing. Rarely challenged at school but
good at gambling. Gadu, the most temperamental of the lot,
easily angry in those early days, but quick to apologize,
quick to repent. Gadu, who was always singing or playing or
teasing or lying, matched against her? With her own quick
impatience, her own way of getting sidetracked on a verse
or a theme. Them—working together?

She looked across at Gadu now. He had settled in his
chair, his head bent, his thick shock of black hair shining, his
wide, bushy eyebrows knit together. His mustache, turning
down like handlebars, almost touched the sprig of black
beard that newly covered his chin. This grown young man in

his late twenties, still temperamental and high-strung, boyish at times, was a son in the faith. Here they were revising the Tboli New Testament together—Gadu working diligently, sometimes needing Maalox to ease his stomach pains, sometimes shutting his eyes tightly to fight the tension headaches that gripped him.

They knew everything about each other, the good and the bad. They argued, fussed, scolded, and shouted at each other. Gadu determined that the book would be natural Tboli. Viv determined that it would be correct exegetically. But their feuding never lasted long. Always they could talk about things, pray about things.

Two hours later, Gadu still remained in the chair across from Viv, a large mug of calamansi juice resting on the table beside him. His eyes were glued to the copy of the Scriptures—his own copy well-marked with minute corrections, with question marks, with added words for clarification. He looked up at Viv, his dark eyes smiling. "This sounds like the old men really talking."

Meanwhile, eight hundred air miles north of Nasuli, behind a post office in the greater Manila area, Mai Tuan faced an insurmountable wall—accusations against his own morality and political integrity. Worse, against his own impregnable, destructive self-image.

Though he denied the accusations against his character, he could not deny the man he had become. Alone in the stockade on the north side of Manila, his body bruised, he looked around. There was no way out of the building, no way to escape his accusers.

He wiped the back of his hand across a shaggy, unkempt beard, touching his dry lips, thinking as he did so how good it would feel to shower, to have a change of clothing, a quick shave.

But even this, he thought, would not change him. He felt

dirty inside, far from God, useless even to himself. The power, the popularity, the prestige, the wealth he had sought had all been his. But this—ten miserable days of confinement. He thrust his clenched hand against the wall of the stockade. His power was being threatened. He pounded furiously with both fists, the echoing sound hitting back at him, mocking him. Mai, the big shot of Kemotu, the boy who had aimed for money, power, and fame, with a goodly portion of each one, was disenchanted. He had hit rock bottom.

Again, needling, restless thoughts gripped him. What would become of him? Where was he heading? He rested his forehead against his hands, his face to the wall. Mai Tuan could not stand himself.

Somewhere there in the loneliness of the stockade, waiting for the next round of interrogation, he cried out in his agony. He couldn't stop crying. Finally, finding the word *God* in his vocabulary, he mouthed it, sensing its strangeness. Then, weeping without tears, he called that Name in earnest.

It was an apologetic prayer at first, a mixture of English and Tboli, a search for words for forgiveness, for guidance, for freedom. It was a plea for another chance, mingled with promises to walk with God again, promises that Mai feared he could never keep.

When he heard the guard coming, he trembled. He did not want to be beaten and questioned again. Suddenly the man stood in the doorway—later Mai would not be able to recall whether it was a guard or an acquaintance—and said blandly, "You are free to go."

Apart from answer to prayer, Mai could not account for his unexpected freedom. As he walked the streets of Manila, heading for that change of clothing and shower, he thought of the Tboli Scriptures. Like Peter he had walked through the open door of a prison. And like Peter he felt new inside.

When rumor of Mai's new commitment to God reached Nasuli, the Tboli team brightened momentarily. Then doubts settled in. Hadn't Mai gone this route before, out of despair, turning back to God? They were afraid to risk becoming vulnerable again by trusting Mai.

Gadu was even more skeptical. In spite of his own explosive personality, he often felt resentful, intimidated, threatened by Mai's rise to power. It would have to be more than a rumor to convince Gadu of a change in Mai. He would have to see for himself.

Weeks later, as Gadu walked the road to Kemotu, he spotted Mai's familiar red truck. Mai slowed his Ford, then stopped altogether. Gadu waited on the edge of the road as Mai stepped from the truck and turned back toward him.

"Na," Mai called, saying in that brief Tboli syllable, "Oh, for goodness' sake, here you are."

Gadu knew that, out of respect, he had to return the greeting. Even as he voiced it, something inside him rebelled, snarled. He stood his ground, studying Mai's face as he approached, noting that there was something different about Mai. His facial lines were tough without harshness. As he came closer, it was obvious to Gadu that Mai was sober. There was no smell of tobacco on him. He walked with a new confidence, the old cockiness gone.

It's true then, Gadu thought, his own facial muscles relaxing. A smile spread over Gadu's triangular face. It was not a smile of cultural politeness or of submission to one in authority. It was Gadu's welcome to a brother in Christ.

By 1978 the Tboli team had scattered. Doris was on a new assignment in Luzon with Judy Wallace, tackling another dialect, "extending the Tboli work to include the Kankanay" as Viv had said. Marge, who would eventually return to the assignment with Doris and Judy among the Kankanay, was in the States, recovering from major cancer surgery. Lil began the new year of 1978 by arriving at Nasuli after months in New York at the bedside of her dying mother. She was back in time for the final proofreading of the Tboli Scriptures. Viv and Gadu had plodded on alone to the completion of the New Testament revision.

There were endless delays. Gadu laid up with a back-ache, a toothache, a cold. Viv procrastinating, striving for perfection in the revision of an already finished manuscript. Team members kept pressuring her from a distance to finish the revision. For Viv there were inner turmoils to contend with—the unbearable thought of leaving the Tboli work for good—as well as the outward preparations for workshops that would enable other teams to complete their own New Testaments at a more rapid pace.

Other colleagues, including Myra Lou Barnard and the former teachers from Nasuli, watched from the sidelines. They could better evaluate the delays, the procrastination, the pushing, the problems as God's instruments of instruction. Surely God wanted the Tboli to be able to read the Scriptures in the language they understood. But didn't he want the Tboli to clearly see him in the lives of those translators who proclaimed his love and power as well? God was polishing his followers—the four team members—by chipping off the rough edges, smoothing out the frictions, conforming them to his image so that Tboli mountain people would find it easy to love the Savior.

At 12:30 P.M. on 13 February 1978, Viv and Gadu dropped their pens on the desk, looked up, smiled, prayed, and gave thanks. They had just finished the last verse in the revision. The Tboli New Testament was ready for printing.

Gadu rocked slightly in the chair across from Vivian. His eyes sparkled. There would be no other outward display of feeling. It was not Tboli to show emotion. "Pray, Ye' Udi," he said quietly.

Viv bowed her head and took a deep breath. "Ma be

longit—Father in Heaven . . . ." She could say no more. Her throat was parched, a lump rising. It was like reaching one's goal after a very long journey. She dissolved in tears.

Gadu leaned back in his chair, threw his head back, and started to laugh—really laugh. "So it is up to me, then?" he teased.

His prayer of thanksgiving poured out. "We are still amazed, Father," Gadu said, "that you chose us to do it. Two people who have been so often disobedient, who have hard heads (stubborn), short breaths (quick tempered), two people who are not quick in their thinking . . . but thanks to the great faithfulness of you, Father, the two such as we were able to finish . . . ."

In the stillness that followed, Viv stood and walked slowly to the open window. She stared out at the familiar hillsides, shadowed in the distance. Around her were large expanses of freshly mowed lawns in a variety of greens. Lush tropical growth—shrubs and flowers bright with color—dotted the neighbors' yards. There was laughter from her colleagues in the house next door. Above her the skies were translucent blue with an endless stretch of fluffy, white clouds, not a sign of a storm to them.

Viv swallowed, reflecting that while God had been at work in individual Tboli lives, he had been at work in the hearts of the team members as well. The birth of a New Testament had stemmed from the growth of a translator. Out of her failures had come successes. Out of her rebellion, obedience. Out of her tears, joy. In the twenty-five years of discovering God's Word in Tboli, she was learning to walk with God.

Inside—deep inside—wave upon wave of joy welled up within her. "Thank you, Father," she whispered again, and then, lest he miss her whispered praise, she shouted it for all Nasuli to hear.

EPILOGUE

Today the bamboo house in the gully stands empty; the roof still leaks. The young men from the household at Sinolon are scattered, some returning to their mountain homes and families. Others, as the team now recognizes, are in strategic positions of leadership, so crucial with the constant unrest around them.

For many of these young men, the glitter of success—the longing to be more than a barefoot mountain boy—has consumed their living. Some have yet to learn that success and progress are available in Jesus Christ. The climb back will be slow and painful. But these boys, these young men, will better understand forgiveness. They will better understand Christ's love. Some of them will yet be a Timothy or a Joshua of Tboli land, youthful examples leading their own people into the promised land.

Someday the house in the gully may completely crumble; the bamboo stakes and trusses that support it may collapse. But God's Word stands sure. Not sin, nor second wives, nor the threat of war can stop the Word of God in Tboli. The Tboli work is God's work. And the nature of God is to endure. When heaven and all earth pass away, God's Word endures forever.